KU-462-764

The Which? Guide to Giving and Inheriting

About the author

Jonquil Lowe is a freelance journalist and former head of the Money Group at *Which?* magazine. She is author of several other *Which?* books on personal finance, including *The Which? Guide to Pensions, Be Your Own Financial Adviser, The Which? Guide to Shares* and *The Which? Guide to Gambling*.

The Which? Guide to Giving and Inheriting

Jonquil Lowe

CONSUMERS' ASSOCIATION

Which? Books are commissioned and researched by
Consumers' Association and published by
Which? Ltd, 2 Marylebone Road, London NW1 4DF
Email address: books@which.net

Distributed by The Penguin Group:
Penguin Books Ltd, 27 Wrights Lane, London W8 5TZ

First edition October 1992
Revised editions June 1994, July 1996
Reprinted September 1996
Revised June 1998
Reprinted January 1999
Revised July 1999

Copyright © 1992, 1994, 1996, 1998, 1999 Which? Ltd

A catalogue record for this book is available from the British Library

ISBN 0 85202 797 4

No part of this publication may be reproduced or transmitted in any form or
by any means, electronically or mechanically, including photocopying,
recording or any other information storage or retrieval system, without prior
permission from the publisher. This publication is not included under licences
issued by the Copyright Agency.

For a full list of Which? books, please write to Which? Books,
Castlemead, Gascoyne Way, Hertford X, SG14 1LH or
access our web site at www.which.net

Cover and text design by Kysen Creative Consultants
Typeset by FMT Colour Ltd
Printed and bound in Great Britain by
Clays Ltd, St Ives plc, Bungay, Suffolk

Contents

★An asterisk next to the name of an organisation in the text indicates that the address can be found in this section.

Whether you are writing your own will or sorting out someone else's will, please note that it is important to consult a legal adviser if substantial sums of money are involved and/or the situation is at all complex.

Introduction

Giving and planning inheritance reflect a natural desire to help kith and kin financially, a philanthropic wish to improve the lot of others and the world in which we live and a determination to pass on hard-won wealth to following generations. The reasons for giving and creating an inheritance may vary but the ultimate goals are the same: to ensure that a gift reaches the right person, is intact and is not squandered or wasted. With a bit of forethought, these goals should be achievable, but too often gifts and inheritance are eroded by unnecessary tax bills and charitable gifts are reduced in value because substantial tax reliefs are overlooked. The message is clear: plan your giving and your gifts will be greater, courtesy of the Inland Revenue.

Planning is also needed to ensure that your gifts reach the right person, especially when it comes to inheritance. Amazingly, only four out of every ten adults in Britain have made wills – and of these nearly one will in five is out of date. Yet without a will you have no say over how your possessions will be passed on. The law takes over and your children could inherit at the expense of your wife or husband, or your wealth could end up in the hands of estranged relatives rather than the people closest to you.

Another advantage of planning is that it can give you some control over how your gifts are used. By giving indirectly through a 'trust', you can build in a variety of conditions. Trusts have a role in both lifetime giving and inheritance. They can be especially useful when making gifts to children or to relatives who are not financially adept.

Since the first edition of this book in 1992, there have been some important developments which – on the face of it – should be good for giving and inheriting. But delve a little deeper and the benefits are less clear-cut. The National Lottery is widely perceived as a good way of benefiting charities, but the proportion of the proceeds going to strictly charitable bodies is much smaller than most people imagine and there is evidence that spontaneous giving has fallen as a direct result of the nation's fascination with the Lottery. The overall impact on charities is estimated as, at best, neutral and, at worst, definitely damaging. Chapter 4 considers whether the Lottery has a valid place in your plan for giving.

Government policy towards giving and inheriting has changed remarkably little. In the run-up to the March 1999 Budget (as in 1998), there were persistent rumours that inheritance tax (IHT) would be overhauled, that rates at which it is charged could soar, that potentially exempt transfers (PETs) would be abolished and that the handing on of business assets and farmland would lose their generous tax reliefs. In the event, it was a very tame Budget. The tax-free slice for inheritance tax was once again increased in line with inflation and the current lenient regime was left intact.

After the major changes to capital gains tax (CGT) the previous year, the March 1999 Budget was a calm affair with little change beyond the annual increase in the tax-free allowance.

Inheritance tax and capital gains tax are the two taxes which will most affect your giving and inheriting, though you should also keep a weather eye on income tax. The ins and outs of these taxes can make giving and inheriting complex and you should be wary of taking any steps in haste – the consequences could be costly. Unless you are certain of your proposed course of action, it usually pays to study the options, to learn how the law affects your plans and to ensure that gifts are carefully documented and legally watertight. With this in mind, Chapter 11 draws together techniques for making tax-efficient lifetime gifts, mirroring Chapter 14 which focuses on strategies for successful inheritance planning.

As in earlier editions, the book uses numerous examples to show you how planned and efficient giving works in practice. In the sections looking at gifts under your will, we have added extensive notes to guide you through this slightly tricky area. Armed with this guide, you should be well on your way to realising your plans to give to charities, family and friends, both in your lifetime and in your will, while avoiding unintentional and unnecessary gifts to the Inland Revenue.

Information in this book generally applies to UK residents making gifts to people, charities and other organisations which are based in the UK. The tax system described here applies throughout the UK. But in some cases, the non-tax rules for Scotland and Northern Ireland differ from those for the rest of the UK; this has been indicated, but details of the different systems are outside the scope of this book.

Changes up to and including the March 1999 Budget have been taken into account, although at the time of writing the Budget proposals have yet to be made law and could be altered.

Chapter 1

Gifts and taxes

Gifts to charity

It is a fortunate paradox that people are willing to give to total strangers through the medium of charities. But, while it is not so odd that we care about, and want to help with, such matters as poverty, suffering, the global standard of living, protecting culture, bio-diversity and saving the environment, it is surely very strange that many people ignore the encouragement which the government offers to charitable giving in the form of tax reliefs.

The British public gives some £5–£6 billion a year to charity.[1] But only three out of every ten households make charitable donations and the vast majority give in a totally unplanned way – responding to door-to-door collections, TV appeals, church collections, sponsoring someone in a fund-raising event, buying a raffle ticket, and so on. In 1997-8, only £1.2 billion of the total charities received from individuals reached them in a tax-efficient way.[2] On tax-efficient gifts by covenant and Gift Aid, charities were able to reclaim £338 million. Higher-rate taxpayers also claimed back some tax on their donations and all taxpayers making charitable donations via the payroll giving scheme benefited from £6 million tax relief. But, with the majority of donations, either the charity, the giver or both missed out on valuable tax reliefs by failing to use these schemes. In the unlikely event that all individual gifts to charity had been made tax-efficiently, charities would have been £1.1–£1.4 billion better off.

With governments shifting ever more responsibility from the public to the voluntary sector, and with the persistent problems of

[1]Charities Aid Foundation (CAF) *Dimensions of the Voluntary Sector 1998*, Kent, CAF, 1998.
[2]Government Statistical Service (GSS) *Inland Revenue Statistics 1998*, London, The Stationery Office, 1998.

droughts and wars in many regions of the world, voluntary donations to charities are increasingly important. It is all the more pressing, therefore, to stop and think about your own charitable giving. Could you plan ahead? For example, could you give fewer larger sums rather than many small donations? Or could you commit yourself to giving regularly? If so, your gifts can be arranged so that the government will add to them and make them even more effective. And your gifts to charities could directly save you tax as well, if they were planned.

Part 1 of this book looks at the range of charitable gifts which may qualify for the available tax reliefs and shows you how to use the special schemes for giving to charity. It also looks at the impact the National Lottery has had on the funding of charities and asks whether playing the Lottery can be viewed as a useful way of helping charities.

Gifts to family and friends

Giving to people you know is not so paradoxical. Most people see themselves as part of a social group and care about the well-being of its members. The most intimate circle is the family, where there is a natural desire to pass on wealth, particularly from one generation to another.

The distribution of wealth

Left unchecked, inheritance within families would, sooner or later, lead to a concentration of wealth in the hands of relatively few people. However, most advanced societies take the view that wealth should not be distributed too unevenly. The reasons for this are varied – political, economic, but also humane. A wide gulf between the poorest people and the richest may encourage political unrest; the votes of relatively poorer people can perhaps be 'bought' by redistributing wealth to them. Economic activity may be improved if wealth is spread more evenly, because of the different spending and saving patterns of the rich and poor.

But there are less pragmatic reasons too. The majority of people want to accumulate enough possessions and wealth to support an enjoyable and sustainable lifestyle, but are not comfortable ignoring the relative, or absolute, poverty of others. Our sense of justice demands that others should also have the chance of a reasonable life.

Yet, even in a society as mature as that of the UK, the distribution of wealth across the population is remarkably uneven, as Table 1.1 (see page 14) shows. Just one-tenth of the adult population in the UK owns half of all the wealth, and a quarter of the population owns nearly three-quarters of all the wealth.

The distribution of wealth is now more even than it was in the early part of the century (see Table 1.2, page 14) which reflects, in part, the deliberate redistribution policies of successive governments. However, there is some evidence that this trend reversed in the early 1990s and that, under the last Conservative government, the gap between rich and poor did widen a little as various lobbying groups have claimed.

The main tool which governments use directly to influence the distribution of wealth is the tax system. Taxes can be used to 'take from the rich' in several ways. One obvious way might be to tax people regularly on the amount of wealth they have. Wealth taxes are used in some countries and have been proposed for the UK in the past.[3] At present in the UK, however, there is no tax on simply *owning* wealth. Instead, the emphasis is on taxing wealth as it changes hands.

Taxing wealth and gifts

Originally, taxing the transfer of wealth was confined to a tax at the time of death and can be traced back to the Anglo-Saxon 'heriot' – a feudal tax paid to the local lord on the death of a tenant. But the modern form of this type of taxation started with estate duty, introduced in 1894 with a swingeing top rate of 8 per cent!

Although estate duty was designed mainly to tax the passing on of wealth at the time of death, it also taxed gifts made in the few years before death to close an otherwise obvious loophole: that is, avoiding the tax through last-minute 'death-bed bequests'. Even so, with planning, it was possible to avoid the worst ravages of the estate duty, particularly by giving away wealth during one's lifetime.

---

[3] *Wealth Tax*, Labour government green paper, London, HMSO, 1974.

Table 1.1 Who owns what in the UK (1995)

Percentage of population[1]	Percentage of wealth owned[2]
1	19
5	38
10	50
25	73
50	92

Notes: [1] Percentage of the most wealthy of the UK adult population.
[2] Percentage of all UK wealth excluding pension rights.
Source: *Inland Revenue Statistics 1998*, London, TSO, 1998.

Table 1.2 Changing fortunes

Year	Percentage of wealth[1] owned by the wealthiest 1%[2]	Percentage of wealth[1] owned by the wealthiest 10%[2]
1911–13	69	92
1924–30	62	91
1936–8	56	88
1954	43	79
1960	38	77
1966	32	72
1972	30	72
1976	21	50
1980	19	50
1985	18	49
1990	18	47
1995	19	50

Notes: [1] Percentage of all UK wealth.
[2] Percentage of the most wealthy of the UK adult population.
Source: *Diamond Commission Initial Report on the Distribution of Income and Wealth*, HMSO, 1975; *Inland Revenue Statistics 1998*, London, TSO, 1998.

In 1975, Harold Wilson's government scrapped estate duty in favour of capital transfer tax. This was a fully fledged gifts tax and estate duty rolled into one. The aim was to tax all transfers of wealth whether made in life or at death – with a few exceptions, such as gifts between husband and wife, small gifts to other people, and up to £2,000 a year (in the 1975–6 tax year) of otherwise taxable transfers. And there were special reliefs to help farmers and businesses. Taxable gifts were added together and the first slice of this total was tax-free. Tax, at progressively higher rates, was levied on subsequent slices until it reached a top rate of 75 per cent. Although this appeared to be a serious tax that would affect even people of relatively modest means, in the event, capital transfer tax lasted only 11 years.

The Conservative government came to power in 1979 determined to reduce the role of the state and encourage individual initiative. Reform of the tax system was an important part of its strategy, and capital transfer tax was on the agenda. In 1986, capital transfer tax was replaced by inheritance tax. In many respects the two taxes are similar, but a major difference is that under the inheritance tax regime most lifetime gifts between people are free from tax, apart from gifts made in the last seven years before the death of the giver. This means that the majority of gifts you make in the course of your day-to-day affairs are not caught up in the inheritance tax net. There has been persistent speculation that the present Labour government will reintroduce taxation of most lifetime gifts but, to date, the current lenient regime has escaped reform.

However, the switch from capital transfer tax to inheritance tax has not been so benign in other ways. Until 1987, inheritance tax, like capital transfer tax and estate duty before it, was levied according to a scale at progressively higher rates. From 14 March 1988 onwards, a single rate of tax (40 per cent on death, 20 per cent during life) has been implemented whatever the scale of the giving. The threshold at which tax starts has been raised substantially with the outcome that many estates are too small to be taxed at all but, where tax does bite, the teeth sink deep.

You may need to watch out for other taxes too. When you give away something (other than cash), you have 'disposed' of it – just as if you had sold it. If the value of the thing has risen since you first acquired it, you will be judged to have made a profit from owning it and there may be capital gains tax to pay – even though you did not actually receive the profit yourself. And income which you give away can sometimes be like a boomerang which keeps coming back to haunt your tax assessments.

Part 2 examines the various taxes you need to watch out for when making gifts in your lifetime and looks at how to arrange your gifts tax efficiently, and Chapter 11 pulls together key tips for planning your lifetime giving. In addition, Part 2 discusses using 'trusts' (special legal arrangements), which can be a way of giving something but retaining some control over how the gift is used. Contrary to popular opinion, trusts are not just for the very wealthy; they can be useful even if you have fairly small sums to give.

As with charitable giving, the pitfalls of the taxes on gifts to family and friends can often be avoided if you plan ahead. Nowhere is this more crucial than in the area of inheritance planning. The first step is, of course, to make a will – though six out of ten people do not even take this step.[4] Yet, without a will, your possessions may not reach the people you want to leave them to and you lose a chance to plan away a possible tax bill.

Part 3 considers the problems of estates where no will is made, explains how gifts made at the time of death are taxed and shows some steps which can be taken to help you develop an effective plan for giving. In the last resort, it may even be possible for your heirs to rearrange gifts made to them under your will (or in accordance with the law if you left no will) and Part 3 also takes a look at how these measures work.

Part 4 draws together some of the issues covered throughout the book which you should consider when contemplating a gift of what is possibly your most valuable asset – your home. Although essentially your home is no different from any other asset, it is often the one which poses the most difficult questions over how best to balance your intention to give against the desire to avoid unnecessary tax.

---

[4] Survey by Mintel, 1995.

Part 1

Giving to charity

Chapter 2

Choosing the charities

'How odd,' said Mary, as she joined the rest of the family around the tea table. 'That phone call was from a man saying he was collecting money for a charity and would I make a donation over the phone with my credit card.'

Mary and Philip support several charities: they respond to regular postal appeals from Help the Aged, buy Christmas gifts through a Save the Children catalogue, belong to the National Trust, and often seek out bargains in the local charity shop. It is likely that their names are on various lists which are passed on to other charities, so Mary was not surprised to be contacted out of the blue. 'But I didn't like to give anything,' she said. 'I've never heard of the charity – though he did say it was registered, whatever that means. I had no way of knowing whether he was genuine . . .'

What is a charity?

Charities are part of the 'voluntary sector' of the economy. The voluntary sector is made up of a very diverse range of organisations – from youth clubs to poverty relief groups, from local fête committees to conservation groups – whose aim is to benefit some specified group or groups of people, or society as a whole. Often voluntary groups are run by lowly paid or unpaid volunteers, but others are large, highly organised concerns with paid workers and well-developed management systems. Voluntary groups often rely on fund-raising, gifts or grants for their finance.

Charities are distinct from the rest of the voluntary sector because they benefit from special tax status which makes them largely exempt from most taxes. There are 187,000 registered charities in England and Wales,[5] and maybe another 100,000 or more which are not registered. A high proportion of these are very small and many are thought to be inactive. In order to be a charity, an organisation must show that its purposes fall into at least one of the following broad areas:[6]

- the relief of poverty
- the advancement of education
- the advancement of religion
- the pursuit of other aims which are judged beneficial to the community.

It is easy to think of examples of charities helping to relieve poverty that fit the first category: Oxfam, Save the Children, Shelter, Help the Aged and so on. People are often surprised, however, at what counts as a charity in the other categories. For example, which of the following do *you* think are charities: ASH, the National Anti-Vivisection Society, the Royal Opera House, the 'Moonies'? Table 2.1 gives you the answers; it shows the results of a survey carried out by *Which?* magazine to test its subscribers' perceptions of which organisations were charities.

The second category of charities – for the promotion of education – is not to be confused with education itself; its scope is much wider and it can cover virtually any field, including medical research, and making available musical and sporting activities, as well as actively passing on skills and knowledge. For example, this category covers charities as diverse as Imperial Cancer Research Fund, the Royal Opera House, Covent Garden, British Red Cross Society, and Action on Smoking and Health (ASH), as well as more obviously educational bodies such as the Pre-school Learning Alliance and a number of schools.

The third category includes bodies such as the Salvation Army, Church Missionary Society, and churches themselves. The final

---

[5] CAF *Dimensions of the Voluntary Sector 1998.*

[6] The division into these broad areas is known as the 'Macnaghten doctrine' after the judge who first defined them.

Table 2.1 *Which?* subscribers' perception of what counts as a charity

Subscribers were asked: which of the following do you think are registered charities?	Percentage of responses			Correct answer
	Yes	No	Don't know	
National Trust	68	16	14	Yes
The Unification Church ('Moonies')	28	47	23	Yes
Anti-apartheid movement	6	54	37	No
Royal Opera House, Covent Garden	27	35	35	Yes
Child Poverty Action Group	73	7	19	Yes
National Anti-Vivisection Society	33	25	39	No
Shelter	82	4	12	Yes
Howard League for Penal Reform	26	20	52	Yes
Eton College	18	47	32	Yes
Action on Smoking and Health (ASH)	21	38	38	Yes
Lord's Day Observance Society	21	30	46	Yes
National Canine Defence League	57	10	30	Yes

Source: *Which?* questionnaire, unpublished, 1990.

category enables charitable status to be given to bodies such as the National Trust, World Wide Fund for Nature and the Royal Society for the Prevention of Cruelty to Animals (RSPCA).

Organisations whose aims are partly or wholly political cannot be charities, even if part of their work falls into one or more of the categories above. But this does not mean that charities have to be totally apolitical. A charity is allowed to try to influence political decisions, but only in the course of pursuing its charitable aims, and it must not be too pro-active in the means it chooses. This is a grey area and even well-established charities have fallen foul of the rules: for example, in 1991, Oxfam was warned that some of its campaigning to relieve distress and suffering in areas such as the Middle East and South Africa had unwittingly strayed too far over the line and amounted to advocating political change, and that in future it would have to curb such political activities.

To clarify the position, in 1995 the Charity Commission★ published guidelines setting out what political activities charities can and cannot participate in. They are allowed to conduct political campaigns, provided the aims are charitable and the campaigns rely on reasoned, rather than emotive, arguments. To this end, charities can analyse and comment on party political electioneering, they can publish the voting records of MPs and they can give supporters ready-made letters to send to MPs or government ministers. Charities must not support any political party and may not participate in party political demonstrations.

What does 'registered' mean?

In general, charities must be registered with the Charity Commission, which is a government body responsible for checking that an organisation's purposes really are charitable, investigating abuse (for example, fraud, or negligent use of charitable funds), and helping charities to operate effectively. But, contrary to popular belief, not all charities must be, or indeed are, 'registered charities'.

Becoming registered is not the same as being granted charitable status. Many types of charities are excluded from the need to register but are still able to benefit from the special tax status. They include universities, voluntary schools, churches, and many very small charities (for which the administrative burden of registration would be ridiculously great given the scale of their activities). Of the registered charities in England and Wales, seven out of every ten have an income of less than £10,000 a year. A further two out of ten have an income of £10,000–£100,000. Only three charities out of every hundred take in more than £1 million a year. But these very large charities account for over three-quarters of all the income going to the registered charities.[7]

Checking out charity collections

Charities raise funds in a wide range of ways: street collections, door-to-door collections, donation boxes in shops and pubs, sponsorships, postal appeals, TV appeals, even telephone appeals.

Though the amounts given are generally small, door-to-door and street collections and buying raffle tickets are probably the most commonly used methods of giving to charity.[8] Whereas you might discard an appeal letter, say, it is hard to refuse a direct appeal for a

[7]CAF *Dimensions of the Voluntary Sector 1998*, Kent, CAF, 1998.
[8]CAF *Dimensions of the Voluntary Sector*, London, CAF, 1995.

small donation, even if you have never heard of the particular charity. So, how can you be sure that the collection is genuinely for charity?

If people arrive at your door collecting money, they must by law carry a collector's certificate of authority (see example overleaf) showing the name, address and signature of the collector, the purpose of the collection and the time period during which the collection is to be made. Similarly, street collectors must carry a written authority from the organisation promoting the collection (which may be the charity or a specialist promoter). Door-to-door collectors and street collectors are also required to wear a prominent badge, which is provided by the charity, while they are collecting (see example overleaf). Do not be afraid to ask to see a collector's authority, and do not give money to anyone who cannot produce such a document.

You might be asked to help with a street or door-to-door collection. Before agreeing, satisfy yourself that the charity is genuine and that you are happy to collect for it. The charity will equip you with your certificate of authority and collector's badge, together with any equipment (e.g. sealed collecting box or envelopes) and instructions to be followed during the collection. These range from the expected, such as always allow donors themselves to put money into the box or envelope, to the bizarre – for example, 'Do not use a pole for a collecting box to reach upper windows or roofs of conveyances'.[9] Other tips to bear in mind are: some dogs really are ferocious – beware; don't take offence if some people ignore you or are downright rude – for every person who rebuffs your approach, there will be others who are very pleased to give and the charity relies on you and other volunteers to do this job. You may be required to deliver the money you collect to a branch member or direct to a bank – the instructions will cover this.

There is no simple way of checking the authenticity of an unsolicited telephone appeal, so you would be wise to be wary of giving by this means. If you want to donate, suggest that the caller sends you a letter identifying the charity and its aims and that you will post any donation you make.

---

[9] British Red Cross Society *Do's and Don'ts for Collectors*, January 1987.

Collector's certificate of authority and badge

HOUSE-TO-HOUSE COLLECTIONS ACT Collector's certificate of authority	HOUSE-TO-HOUSE COLLECTIONS ACT
NAME *Ivor Pound* OF *Penny Hill, Castle Canton* is hereby authorised to collect for XYZ SOCIETY FOR THE RELIEF OF POVERTY 44 Almshouse Lane, London, NW10 IN *Penny Hill* DURING THE PERIOD *5–11 May 1999* Signed *I M Shakepot* Director Signature of Collector *Ivor Pound*	**XYZ SOCIETY FOR THE RELIEF OF POVERTY** AUTHORISED COLLECTOR'S BADGE Signature of collector *Ivor Pound* **A registered charity**

Checking out the charities

You can check whether an organisation is a registered charity by consulting the Central Register of Charities kept by the Charity Commission for England and Wales.★ If you want to check the more detailed file held about a particular charity, you will need to give the office two to three days' notice.

The computer entry on the Register will tell you the charity's registration number, its address and briefly what the charity does. If an organisation is on the Register, you can treat this as confirmation that it is indeed a charity.

The Charity Commission cannot usually help if your enquiry concerns a charity that is not registered, but there are a number of bodies which may be able to provide information about both registered and non-registered charities. To know whether or not an organisation has been granted charitable status, contact the Charity Division of the Inland Revenue.★

Your local authority will usually have details of charities operating in your area, and may have its own register which you can inspect.

The Charities Aid Foundation (CAF)★ – which is itself a charity, whose general aim is to promote growth in the flow of resources to the voluntary sector – operates a Charity Search service which can give you information about a specific charity or identify charities operating in a particular area or for a given cause.

Directories are produced by various organisations representing voluntary groups – not only charities. These organisations may be able to put you in touch with local sources of information about the charities in your area, and give you details of charities and other groups involved in particular activities or places.

The national bodies to contact for further information are the National Council for Voluntary Organisations for England, the Northern Ireland Council for Voluntary Action,* the Wales Council for Voluntary Action* and the Scottish Council for Voluntary Organisations.*

But where does the money go?

Bear in mind that, although an organisation may be a charity, neither charitable status nor registration represents a 'seal of approval'. You may still want to satisfy yourself that any money you give will be used efficiently and as you had expected. Unfortunately, there is no easy way of checking this, but a charity's financial accounts will give you some information.

All charities (whether registered or not) must prepare annual accounts describing the financial affairs of the charity over the year. They must provide you with a copy of these accounts within two months of your written request – the charity can charge you a reasonable fee for doing this. Many registered charities are required by law to provide the Charity Commission with copies of their accounts. Where accounts have been submitted to the Commission, they are available for the public to inspect. You can also glean much useful information about the 500 largest charities[10] from an annual CAF publication, *Dimensions of the Voluntary Sector*, which can be found in some public libraries or bought from CAF.

A charity's accounts will give you, *inter alia*, some idea about how the charity uses the funds it raises. One area of particular concern is how much of your money actually reaches the charitable cause. Inevitably, some funds must be spent on organising and running the charity itself. Research by CAF suggests people fear that nearly half of their donations might be going to pay for administration, whereas, on average, it was felt that less than a fifth should be used up in this

---

[10]'Largest' in terms of income from fund-raising.

way.[11] Interestingly, data collected by CAF show that non-charitable spending by the top 500 charities is much lower than feared. In 1996–7, 69 per cent of the spending of the top 500 charities was 'direct charitable expenditure'. A further 6.5 per cent was paid out in grants to other organisations and to individuals. The remaining 24 per cent was split between fundraising and publicity (9 per cent), management and administration (4 per cent) and shop/trading expenses (11 per cent). Inevitably, there was a widespread variation between individual charities with, for example, management and administration costs ranging from less than 1 per cent of total income up to 60 per cent.[12] However, you need to take care when interpreting cost figures. A high level of costs may indeed suggest inefficiency, but equally a low level of costs may be the result of the charity spending too little on administration and management. And a charity which has as its main activity giving advice, say, rather than passing on funds may justifiably have high running costs.

[11]CAF *Individual Giving and Volunteering in Britain. Who gives what . . . and why,* 5th ed. Tonbridge, CAF, 1992.
[12]CAF *Dimensions of the Voluntary Sector 1998*, Kent, CAF, 1998.

Chapter 3

Special schemes for giving to charity

GIVE MORE, PAY THE SAME

'Look, here's another appeal from the Salvation Army.' Philip passed the envelope across to his wife, Mary. 'We must give something,' she said. 'Oh, did you see this?' Mary held up a pink leaflet headed *Covenanting your £10-a-month gift could increase its value to £12.99 at no extra cost to you.* 'It says the Chancellor will add the extra, but we'd have to keep on donating for four years – well, since we give to them regularly anyway, it seems churlish not to accept the Chancellor's offer!'

Tax benefits for charities

The great advantage to an organisation of having charitable status is that it becomes eligible for a variety of tax benefits. As long as they meet certain conditions, charities currently enjoy complete freedom from income tax, capital gains tax and corporation tax on their income and profits from most sources. In addition, when they receive donations, charities may be able to claim back income tax which has been paid by the giver (see below).

Whereas most businesses must pay business rates to their local authority, charities are given automatic relief against four-fifths of these rates, and the local authority can exempt them from the remaining fifth if it chooses.

Charities are not completely free from tax; they are, in the main, treated like any other business when it comes to Value Added Tax (VAT). This can be a problem, especially for charities whose activities count as exempt from VAT, since they cannot reclaim VAT paid on a wide range of items that they buy. Some things charities need – for example, equipment to be used for medical research, new building for charitable purposes, and provision of toilet facilities in buildings run by charities for charitable purposes – can be purchased VAT-free. Spending on advertising is also normally VAT-free for charities.

Many charities receive dividends from funds which they invest in shares. Dividends are received after deduction of income tax together with a tax credit. Charities used to be able to reclaim the amount of the tax credit, so dividend income was tax-free. From 6 April 1999, the position changed. Charities are no longer be able to reclaim the tax already deducted. However, to help them adjust, they receive compensation from the government for the lost tax credit. The compensation is given at a reducing rate over a five-year period, coming to an end in tax year 2003–4.

The taxation of charities, particularly the problems posed by VAT, is at the time of writing the subject of a government review and consultation.

Advantages for donors

If you make *ad hoc* donations to charity, there is usually no tax benefit to either you or the charity. But several special schemes are in operation which will give you tax relief either directly or indirectly by increasing the value of your gifts to charity. Non-taxpayers, however, should avoid these schemes because they could end up with an unexpected bill from the Inland Revenue – so watch out, especially if your income varies a lot.

The government's review of charity taxation (see above) is also considering how the tax reliefs available to donors can be improved to encourage more people to give. The various schemes currently available and the improvements the government is suggesting are described in the following sections.

Deed of covenant

A deed of covenant is a legally binding written promise. You agree to pay the charity a given sum of money on a regular basis. The advantage of giving in this way is that the charity can receive more than you actually give. You can use a deed of covenant to make regular gifts of any size you wish to any registered charity.

By making payments through a deed of covenant, technically you are transferring part of your income to the charity. As such, you are also allowed to 'transfer' the tax bill associated with that income. This means that as long as you are a taxpayer, you qualify for tax relief on the amount you give to the charity. In practice, you hand over a 'net' sum to the charity – an amount from which tax at the basic rate (23 per cent in the 1999–2000 tax year) has already been deducted. You keep the tax deducted which provides you with tax relief at the basic rate. For example, suppose you would like a charity to receive £100 a year. Instead of handing over a full £100, you keep back £23 as tax relief at the basic rate, giving the charity the remaining £77.

EXAMPLE 3.1

In June 2000, Mary thought she would like the Salvation Army to receive £100 a year from her through a deed of covenant. She is a basic-rate taxpayer, so she could achieve this in the first year by agreeing to hand over £77 – i.e. £100 less tax relief at the basic rate for 1999–2000, which was 23 per cent. The charity would reclaim the £23 from the Inland Revenue, bringing the total it receives up to £100. But in 2000–1 the basic tax rate is due to fall to 22 per cent. Because Mary is paying under a 'net covenant' (see page 30), she will continue to pay an after-tax-relief amount of £77. But the Salvation Army will get back a little less in reclaimed tax – only £21.72, bringing the total to be received in 2000–1 to £98.72.

Philip suggests that he should make the family's donation to the Salvation Army, rather than Mary, because he is a higher-rate taxpayer and would qualify for more tax relief. If he had been the donor from the start, like Mary, he would have handed over £77 each year to the charity, which would have reclaimed basic-rate tax, bringing the total donation to £100 in year 1 and £98.72 from year 2. Philip would then have given details of the donation on his tax return and reclaimed further tax relief of 17 per cent (40 per cent less the 23 per cent basic rate) in 1999–2000 and 18 per cent (40 per cent less 22 per cent) in 2000–1. This comes to £17 in 1999–2000 and £17.77 in 2000–1. This means that it would have cost Philip just £60 in year 1 to give the charity £100 and £59.23 in year 2 to give £98.72. His extra tax relief would have been given to him through his pay by adjusting his PAYE code.

If you are a higher-rate taxpayer, there is more tax relief due to you that you must reclaim directly from the Inland Revenue.[13] Normally, you do this after the end of the tax year by giving details of your covenant payments to charity on your tax return. The Inland Revenue will then either send you a cheque or adjust your PAYE code or tax bill as appropriate. The charity is exempt from income tax and so can claim back from the Inland Revenue the tax you have deducted, thus boosting the size of your gift.

To qualify for special tax treatment, you must intend to make covenanted payments to the charity for at least four years. But it is unlikely that a charity would insist that you keep up the payments if, say, you fell on hard times.

Often a charitable covenant will specify that payments are to be made for four years or until some later event, such as giving up membership of the charity. In the past, such a covenant ceased to be effective at the end of four years and the charity concerned would have to ask you to renew your covenant. But, since 1992, covenants with this type of wording can automatically continue to be valid.

To satisfy the tax rules, the wording of a deed of covenant must be very precise. Fortunately, you do not need to worry about this, because nearly all charities will gladly provide you with a suitable covenant form (an example is shown opposite). You just need to add the relevant details and your signature. In England, Wales and Northern Ireland, you will need someone to witness your signature. (In Scotland, you will need either two witnesses or none at all, but where you do not have witnesses you must write 'Adopted as holograph' above your signature.)

The example of a covenant (opposite) is a 'net covenant': that is, you agree to hand over a fixed sum of money to the charity each year. If the basic tax rate changed (as in Example 3.1 on page 29), you would still hand over the same amount, but the charity would reclaim a different amount of tax. More rarely, you might use a 'gross covenant' to make charitable gifts; with this, you agree to give the charity a fixed *before-tax* sum. If the basic tax rate changes, the amount you hand over to the charity also changes – but so does the amount of tax relief the charity reclaims, so the charity continues to receive the same total (gross) sum.

[13]But if a charity uses part of a covenanted gift for non-charitable purposes (other than meeting reasonable administration costs), higher-rate tax relief may be reduced or even withdrawn completely.

EXAMPLE OF A COVENANT TO CHARITY

DEED OF COVENANT

I ———— (your name) of ———— (your address) undertake to pay ———— (name of charity) each year for four years (or during my lifetime if shorter) the sum that will after deduction of income tax at the basic rate be £———— (amount you want to give) from ———— (date of first payment).

Signed and delivered by ———— (your signature)
Date ———— (date you sign the covenant)

Witness's signature ————
Witness's address ————

If you are interested in giving by covenant, there are a few points to watch out for, as follows:

- a covenant cannot be backdated, so make sure that the first payment under it falls due *after* the covenant has been signed
- if you are a non-taxpayer in any year when a payment is made under the covenant, the charity will still be able to claim tax relief, but the Inland Revenue will then ask you to hand over a sum equal to the tax relief given. Similarly, if you are a lower-rate taxpayer, you will have to pay the Revenue part of the tax relief given to the charity. So, if you are a non-taxpayer or lower-rate taxpayer or expect to become one during the course of the covenant's life, do not make gifts to charity in this way
- a covenant is not normally valid if you receive something in return for making the payments.

This last point can be a problem for charities which offer various benefits to subscribing members: for example, magazines, free use of premises, or free entry to otherwise commercial events. As the law stands, a covenant can be used to pay the subscription only if any benefits to the members are minimal; in other cases, the covenant would not be valid and the special tax treatment would not apply. There is an exception: a covenant is a valid way of paying the subscription to a charity which gives free or reduced-rate admission to properties preserved for the public benefit or places where wildlife is conserved for the public benefit. This means, for example, that members of the National Trust can pay their subscription by covenant.

In the 1997–8 tax year, £1,125 million was given to charities through deeds of covenant including the value of the basic-rate tax reclaimed. The total cost of tax relief on covenants to charity was £310 million in that year.[14]

EXAMPLE 3.2

Harold likes to support charities when he can afford to. He works for himself and his income is a bit erratic, so he has never liked the idea of committing himself to regular donations. But, at present, work is going well, and he has decided to make a gift of £200 to a local charity running a hospice for people who are terminally ill. If he pays the £200 using a loan covenant, the charity will actually receive £257.24 in total, assuming a basic tax rate 23 per cent in 1999–2000 and 22 per cent thereafter. The scheme works as shown in the table below (Harold is definitely expected to earn enough to be a basic-rate taxpayer throughout the next four years). From 2001, Harold may be able to use the Gift Aid scheme instead (see page 34).

Year	1999–2000	2000–1	2001–2	2002-3
Harold makes a loan to the charity	£200			
Charity repays the loan	£50	£50	£50	£50
Payments under the deed of covenant (financed by the loan repayments)	£50	£50	£50	£50
Basic-rate tax relief reclaimed by the charity on the covenant payments[1]	£14.94	£14.10	£14.10	£14.10
Total received by the charity	£64.10	£64.10	£64.10	£64.10

[1]Assuming basic-rate tax is 23 per cent in 1999-2000 and 22 per cent in subsequent years.

[14]*Inland Revenue Statistics 1998*, London, TSO, 1998.

If you are an employee and a higher-rate taxpayer and you want to give no more than £100 a month to charity, consider 'Payroll Giving' (see page 38) instead of using a covenant (if your employer operates a scheme). With Payroll Giving, you get all the tax relief due to you at the time you make your gift rather than having to wait for the higher-rate relief.

If you want to give at least £100 to a charity dealing with overseas poverty or education issues, you may be able to use the Millennium Gift Aid scheme (page 37). From 2001, this could be extended to cover all charities – see page 36.

In the government's review of charity taxation, charities pointed out that covenants are a very important source of donations and the most widely used of the special schemes available. But there is a lot of administrative work involved, some people may be put off by the need to commit themselves to giving for several years, and it can be hard for charities to persuade people to renew their covenants once the four-year period is up. The government considered whether the system could be simplified and made more accessible but decided that the best way forward was to develop the Gift Aid system (see page 34) as a modern alternative to covenants rather than changing the covenant system.

Loan covenant

A loan covenant (also called a 'deposited covenant' or 'deposited deed') is a way of donating a lump sum to a charity but still benefiting from the tax advantages of a covenant. You agree to give money to a charity under a normal deed of covenant lasting, say, four years. But, at the same time, you make an interest-free loan to the charity which is to be repaid in four yearly instalments. The loan repayments are used to make the gifts under the covenant. As each covenant payment is made, the charity can claim back tax in the normal way – and you can claim higher-rate tax relief on the covenant payments in any year in which you are a higher-rate taxpayer.

Loan covenants can be used to make lump-sum gifts of any size, but the administration costs involved mean that gifts below, say, £100 are not worthwhile via this route. And bear in mind that tax relief for the charity and for higher-rate taxpayers is spread over the lifetime of the covenant. If you want to give £250 or more you should instead choose the 'Gift Aid' scheme (see below); with this scheme tax relief is given straight away. If you want to donate a smaller sum (but still £100 or more) to third-world charities, you may be able to use the Millennium Gift Aid scheme (see page 37) which was introduced on 31 July 1998.

Gift Aid

You can use Gift Aid to make fairly large lump-sum gifts to charity. The scheme is rather similar to using a covenant in that you hand over a sum which is deemed to be net of basic-rate income tax. The charity can then reclaim the tax deducted. If you are a higher-rate taxpayer, you can claim higher-rate tax relief direct from your tax office. Usually, you will do this after the end of the tax year in which you make the gift by filling in the appropriate section of your tax return.

To use Gift Aid, the net sum you give must be £250 or more for payments made on or after 16 March 1993. (The limit was £400 before that date and £600 before 7 May 1992.) If you make a gift jointly with other people – your husband or wife, say, or work colleagues – you can still use Gift Aid as long as your share of the gift is £250 or more. There is no upper limit to the amount you can donate.

EXAMPLE 3.3

Following the death of a close friend from cancer, Philip gives £770 to the Imperial Cancer Research Fund in 1999–2000 using the Gift Aid scheme. The charity is able to reclaim basic-rate tax of £230, bringing the total it receives to £1,000. Philip reclaimed higher-rate relief of £170 (17 per cent of £1,000) from his tax office. This means that Philip paid just £600 to make a gift of £1,000 to the charity.

There are several points to watch out for when considering using the Gift Aid scheme, as follows:

- if you are a non-taxpayer, the charity will still be able to claim tax relief but the Inland Revenue will ask you for a sum equal to the amount of relief given. Similarly, the Revenue will demand part of the tax relief from you if you are a lower-rate taxpayer

Single Donation of Gift Aid

Inland Revenue

Certificate of single payment by an individual to a charity

For completion by the donor	Complete in CAPITAL letters

I CERTIFY

- that I *Enter your initials and surname*

  P. H. BROWN

  Enter the charity name

  have made a single payment to   IMPERIAL CANCER RESEARCH FUND

  Enter the sum paid to the charity: not less than £250

  in the sum of   £ 770 —   — p

Day	Month	Year

  on   10   04   99

- and that I am resident in the United Kingdom and have paid or will pay basic rate income tax on the gross amount of the gift   See NOTE A overleaf
- and that the payment – was made in money and was not subject to a condition that any part of it can be repaid
  – was not due under a deed of covenant nor was it paid under a payroll giving scheme
  – was not paid for any benefits beyond the limits described overleaf   See NOTE B overleaf
  – was not linked with the acquisition of property by the charity except by gift   See NOTE C overleaf

ALL OF THE ABOVE CONDITIONS MUST BE SATISFIED FOR THE PAYMENT TO QUALIFY FOR TAX RELIEF

Signature   Philip Brown   Date   1 / 5 / 99

Address   10 NEW STREET
NEWTOWN
SOMERSET

Postcode   AB1 CD2

Return your completed Certificate to the CHARITY

For completion by the charity

Charity claims reference number ....

Donation record number ....

For completion by Inland Revenue

Donor record traced ....   Tax Office notified

Address ....   Other action ....

R190(SD)

- 35

- you cannot combine Gift Aid with any of the other tax-advantageous ways of giving to charity. So, for example, you cannot use a Gift Aid donation to finance a series of covenant payments
- the tax advantages will be withdrawn if you (or anyone connected with you, such as family or close business associates) receive anything more than a purely token benefit in return for the donation (taken to mean anything exceeding in value 2.5 per cent of your donation). This means that, for example, you cannot use Gift Aid to pay subscriptions, school fees, or to buy a season ticket for the opera.

Either when you hand over your gift or soon after, you must also give the charity a completed **form R190(SD)** – see page 35 – which certifies that your payment is eligible for the scheme. The charity can provide you with this form. If you do not complete an R190(SD), the charity will not be able to claim tax relief. From 1999, the form has been made easier to complete by no longer requiring details of your National Insurance number or income tax reference. The government is also looking into other ways to cut the paperwork – for example, allowing you to give details over the phone instead if you are making a donation by phone or allowing an electronic version of the form if you are giving by Internet.

The Gift Aid scheme has been running since 1 October 1990 and, up to March 1998, a total of £1,165 million had been given in this way by individual donors. Charities were able to reclaim tax relief of £380 million on this sum, bringing the total raised through Gift Aid to £1,545 million.[15]

As part of its review of charity taxation, the government is looking at how Gift Aid might be developed to encourage more donations to be made by this route. The current £250 minimum donation is higher than the amount many people can afford or want to give. Millennium Gift Aid (see opposite) caters for smaller donations. The government is monitoring the experience of Millennium Gift Aid and has suggested that, if the scheme proves popular, ordinary Gift Aid could be developed along the same lines. In other words, the minimum donation would fall to £100 and a series of smaller gifts totalling £100 would qualify. The government has indicated that these changes could be made from 2001.

---

[15]*Inland Revenue Statistics 1998*, London, TSO, 1998.

Millennium Gift Aid

In the March 1998 Budget, the government announced a special extension of the Gift Aid scheme to mark the millennium. From 31 July 1998 up to 31 December 2000, gifts as small as £100 will qualify for Gift Aid tax reliefs, provided they are made to participating charities which support education and anti-poverty programmes in the world's poorest countries. A series of gifts where the instalments total £100 or more will also qualify. Charities will be able to tell you whether or not they are participating in the scheme.

The countries concerned are those which have been designated as 'low-income countries' by the World Bank. They are mainly in Asia and Africa and include, for example, Azerbaijan, Bosnia, Burundi, India, Pakistan, Rwanda, Vietnam and Zambia.

Tax relief will be given in the same way as for the main Gift Aid scheme described on page 34.

When you make your gift to the charity, you should state that you wish to use the Millennium Gift Aid scheme. The charity will then send you **form R190(MGA)** to complete and return to the charity. If you are making a series of smaller gifts, you fill in the form when your last gift has brought the total to £100 or more.

The government is to run a publicity campaign under the name Gift Aid 2000 to encourage people to use the Millennium Gift Aid scheme.

EXAMPLE 3.4

Martin has always been a keen supporter of charities, such as Oxfam, which aim to relieve poverty in the Third World. He regularly responds to their collections and mail shots but has never felt able to give enough to make use of the various tax-efficient schemes for donating. But he could just afford a one-off donation of £100 later in 1999. The charity would be able to reclaim tax at the basic rate of £29.87 bringing the total value of the donation to £129.87. Martin is a basic-rate taxpayer, so he cannot claim any further relief himself.

Payroll Giving schemes

Payroll Giving (also called 'Payroll Deduction') is a method of making regular gifts to charity out of your pay-packet. It is open only to employees, and only to those whose employer operates a Payroll Giving scheme. From 1996–7 onwards, you can give any amount up to a maximum of £1,200 in total during the tax year (£100 a month). Prior to 6 April 1996 the limit was £900 a year and before 6 April 1993 the limit was £600.

The scheme works like this. Your employer sets up an arrangement with an agency approved by the Inland Revenue (in fact, a few employers have set up their own agencies). You then tell your employer how much you want to give each payday and to which charity or charities. The employer deducts the specified amount from your pay and hands it over to the agency, which arranges for the money to be transferred to the charities you picked. (The agency may make a charge – for example, 5 per cent of the donations it handles – to cover its own running costs, but sometimes there is no charge or your employer might separately cover any administration costs.) Your donation is deducted from your pay before tax (but not National Insurance) is worked out, so you automatically get full income tax relief. Payroll Giving is popular with charities because they receive the whole (gross) donation direct from you, avoiding any paperwork and delay involved in claiming tax relief from the Inland Revenue.

One of the largest agencies running Payroll Giving schemes is the Charities Aid Foundation (CAF),★ which operates a scheme called Give As You Earn (GAYE). It offers four different options:

- *Elective scheme* Each employee chooses up to eight charities to receive his or her donation each month
- *Charity account* Donations are paid into a special account from which you can make donations of any size to any charities. See page 48 for more details
- *Staff charity fund* Employees pool their individual donations to form a single account from which donations of any size can be made to any charities
- *Matched giving* The employer agrees to match pound for pound the donations of the employees, usually up to a given limit, such as £250 per employee per year.

EXAMPLE 3.5

Mary earns £700 a month, before tax, working in the local branch of a national building society. The society operates a Payroll Giving scheme through which Mary gives £10 a month each to Help the Aged and Barnardo's. Normally, Mary would pay £73.22 a month in income tax (during the 1999–2000 tax year), but after deducting the Payroll Giving from her pay, the tax bill is reduced to £68.62 a month. In other words, she gets tax relief of £4.60, which reduces the cost to her of the £20 she gives to charity to just £15.40.

If your employer operates a Payroll Giving scheme, he or she can provide you with details and an application form.

You do not have to keep up your donations for any minimum period of time. You stop making them whenever you like simply by informing your employer of your wishes.

Payroll Giving cannot be used in combination with any of the other tax-advantageous ways of giving to charity. So, for example, you cannot make gifts under a deed of covenant through a Payroll Giving scheme. Inland Revenue rules do not allow Payroll Giving to be used to pay subscriptions entitling you, for example, to membership benefits from a charity.

Payroll Giving was introduced in April 1987. The amount donated by this route has increased gradually but steadily and stood at £27 million in the 1997–8 tax year, on which tax relief of £6 million was given. Some 370,000 people currently donate by this route.[16] About 9,000 Payroll Giving schemes are in operation.[17]

Compared with the amount donated through covenants, say, the overall level of donations through Payroll Giving is disappointing. The government estimates that fewer than one in 100 employers operate a scheme and fewer than two in every 100 employees give this way. But it believes that, with better promotion and incentives, Payroll Giving could become much more important.

In its review of charity taxation, the government has made various suggestions for improving Payroll Giving by, for example, raising the

---

[16]*Inland Revenue Statistics 1998*, London, TSO, 1998.

[17]HM Treasury *Review of Charity Taxation: consultation document*, London, HM Treasury, March 1999.

ceiling on donations or removing it altogether, allowing employers to pass on donations direct to charities rather than through an agency, and embarking on a major publicity campaign. Another idea is for the government to add a supplement (of, say, 10 per cent) to donations made through Payroll Giving for a period of perhaps two or three years, just to 'kick-start' the scheme.

US-style giving

The government's review of charity taxation has also looked at the system used in the USA. There, whatever scheme you use, you make gross donations to charity and all the tax relief goes direct to you, not to the charity. You claim the relief on all your donations through your tax return and you can make gifts up to 30 per cent or 50 per cent (depending on the type of gift and type of charity) of your yearly before-tax income.

The government decided that such a system would not be practical across the board in the UK, where far fewer people than in the USA fill in tax returns each year. But it could perhaps be introduced for those people who regularly receive a tax return, such as the self-employed and higher-rate taxpayers.

Chapter 4

The National Lottery

ALL IN A GOOD CAUSE

'Of course, we shan't win,' Mary sighed as she handed her Lottery card to the cashier. 'Why do you buy Lottery tickets then, Mummy?' quizzed Jessica. 'Well, there's always that small, tantalising chance,' replied Mary. 'Though the chance of winning the jackpot is tiny, there's no chance at all of winning if we don't buy a ticket. Besides, we're helping charity – some of the money we pay for tickets is passed on to all sorts of good causes.' 'How much?' Jessica wondered. 'I'm not absolutely sure, darling, but it's quite a lot, I think . . .'

A survey by the National Council for Voluntary Organisations (NCVO)* in 1996 found that on average people thought more than 18p from each £1 Lottery ticket went to charity.[18] In fact, the amount is much lower – around 5p. Even so, that's a large amount of cash, because so many people play. Each week around three-quarters of all households in the UK (some 30 million people) play the National Lottery draw game. On average, each person spends £3.15 a week on the main draw games (held on Saturdays and Wednesdays) and £1.50 on the scratchcard games, called Instants. Since the start of the Lottery in November 1994 up to May 1999, it had raised over £6.75 billion for 'good causes'.[19] Not surprisingly, over half the people interviewed in the NCVO survey thought that playing the Lottery was a good way of giving to charity. But charities themselves

---

[18]National Council for Voluntary Organisations *Charitable Giving in Great Britain 1996*, London, NCVO, 1997.

[19]National Lottery Internet site.

have reason to be less happy with this popular national sport.

Where the money goes

For more than a century, lotteries were illegal in Britain. Then, the Betting and Lotteries Act 1934 allowed two small concessions – private lotteries among people who were members of the same club or working together, say, and incidental lotteries run at fêtes and similar events but offering small prizes valued at no more than £10. Throughout the 20th century, there has been a gradual shift to permitting a wider spread of lotteries and slightly more tempting prizes, but prior to the National Lottery the top prize any legal lottery could offer was just £2,000 – a sum which was dwarfed by the potential winnings from other forms of gambling, such as the football pools. Britain's stance was at odds with its Continental neighbours, which all raise money through national lotteries, as do many other countries around the world ranging from India to Australia. After much debate, the National Lottery Act was passed in 1993 and the first Lottery draw took place on Saturday 19 November 1994 with a jackpot prize of over £2 million. The Lottery was an immediate success. Within 12 hours of the Lottery terminals going live, more than seven million tickets had been sold. Since then the range of Lottery games has expanded with the addition of instant-win scratchcards and the mid-week prize draw. It is estimated that nine out of ten adults in Britain have bought a Lottery ticket at least once – one of the highest participation rates in the world.

The National Lottery is managed under licence on the government's behalf by a commercial company. Only one company at a time can run the Lottery – at present, this company is Camelot. On average, out of every £1 of Lottery income, 4p goes to Camelot and a further 5p goes to the retailers who run Lottery terminals. The government takes 13p in tax. Half the fund is paid out in prizes, leaving about 28p in the pound to be distributed to the 'good causes', but in 1996–7 some 30p in the pound went to the good causes. Originally, there were five good causes, but these have since been expanded to six. Table 4.1 shows how the different good causes share the Lottery revenue.

On average then, the National Lottery Charities Board receives about 4.7p for every Lottery ticket sold. This gives an idea of the amount of Lottery money going to charity, but is not precise because:

Table 4.1 How the 'good causes' share their Lottery revenues

Good cause[1]	Distribution administered by:	% of the 'good cause' fund
Charities	National Lottery Charities Board	16.67%
The arts	Arts councils	16.67%
Sport	Sports councils	16.67%
National heritage	National Heritage Memorial Fund	16.67%
Projects to mark the millennium	The Millennium Commission	20%
Health, education and environmental projects	New Opportunities Fund (NOF)	13.33%

[1] In addition, a new National Endowment for Science, Technology and the Arts (NESTA) is expected to receive a lump sum endowment from the Lottery as well as raising funds from other sources.

- the Charities Board can make grants to benevolent and philanthropic organisations which fall outside the legal definition of 'charity' provided they have 'the essential attributes of charity' and meet various other requirements
- the legal definition of 'charity' is very wide (see Chapter 2). Some of the arts, sports and other bodies which receive funds from the various lottery money distributors also have charitable status.

How the Charities Board shares out the funds

In the Charities Board's own words: 'The primary aim of the National Lottery Charities Board is to give grants to help meet the needs of those at greatest disadvantage in society and to improve the quality of life in the community.' In the past, it has done this by picking a different theme for each round of funding and inviting applications by a specified closing date. Themes have, for example, included poverty, youth issues, health and disability, and so on. Applications from projects which did not fit in with the theme were considered only in exceptional circumstances. Now, the Board has a more varied system, mixing themed rounds with open-ended funding programmes. Table 4.2 summarises the Charities Board's grant programmes for 1999.

Table 4.2 National Lottery Charities Board funding programmes for 1999

Main grants programmes

Community	Continuous – no closing date
Poverty and disadvantage	Continuous – no closing date

Small grants

Called Awards for All in England and Scotland and Small Grants Celebrating the Millennium in Wales and Northern Ireland. Grants from £500 to £15,000; small organisations (income less than £15,000 a year) take priority	Continuous – no closing data. Joint scheme with the other 'good causes'

Funding rounds with deadlines

International (aimed at organisations working abroad)	Opens autumn 1999
Health and social research	Grants will be announced summer 2000

The Charities Board gives both capital grants and funding for on-going expenses. Unlike some of the other sources of funding (e.g. the Sports Councils), charities do not have to raise part of the funding for a project themselves. The Board's grants are not meant to replace statutory funding for a project – in other words, money which would otherwise have been provided by national or local government or a similar body. The projects it has supported are many and varied: for example, £500 to a toy library in Swindon to buy multi-cultural toys; £30,000 to the Stafford Swallows Sports Club for the Disabled to buy a specially adapted minibus; £454,948 to the Kids' Club Network to support a nationwide project to set up out-of-school clubs; £173,483 to the Pooh Bear Reading Assistance Society to tackle child and adult illiteracy in the Hull region; £66,540 to Links Housing Group to provide an advice and support service for young people in need of housing in the Tynedale area of Northumberland; £119,889 to Saheh in Manchester, a refuge for Asian women and children fleeing from domestic violence; £86,541 to Usk House Day Hospice; and £16,025 to Radio Lollipop to bring volunteer-run radio stations into hospitals in Scotland.

Why are charities unhappy?

With such a successful and lucrative source of funding, it may seem surprising that charities themselves have not been wholehearted supporters of the Lottery. But the money which people spend on Lottery tickets has to come from somewhere and it seems that more direct forms of giving to charity are suffering. Surveys by the CAF* and NCVO suggest that the proportion of people making donations to charity was 13 per cent lower in 1996 than in 1993, with only two-thirds of the adult population now giving to charity. This compares with a peak of 81 per cent of all adults in pre-Lottery days. The research shows that donations slumped particularly badly in the months when the Lottery jackpot was very high because of 'double rollovers'. NCVO claims that this indicates a clear relationship between the success of Lottery ticket sales and the decline in charitable giving. NCVO research found that voluntary donations to charity amounted to £4.58 billion in 1996 – down 20 per cent from their 1993 level of £5.7 billion. The average monthly donation had fallen from £10.08 in 1993 to £8.69 in 1996. However, separate research by Barings Asset Management into the top 3,000 charities found little evidence of the Lottery squeezing donations, so the picture is not clear-cut and the impact on different charities seems to vary.

Hardest-hit have been those charities which rely on traditional methods of fund-raising, such as street collections and their own lotteries and raffles. The Welsh-based medical research charity Tenovus is one example. In March 1995, it announced that it was closing down the scratchcard lottery which it had run for 15 years through various outlets, including supermarkets. Proceeds of its lottery had already slumped since the launch of the National Lottery, but the introduction of the National Lottery's own scratchcards in that month proved fatal. Tenovus, with its top prize of £5,000 or a car, simply could not compete with Lottery Instants' £50,000 jackpot.

The problems for individual charities were initially made worse because of the Charities Board's system of themed funding rounds. A charity which was losing money because of competition from the Lottery might have waited some time before a theme relevant to its own project work came round and provided an opportunity to apply for a Charities Board grant. The position has now improved. The Charities Board took some time to get going, and the first allocations of grants were made only in 1995. From 1996 onwards, any decrease in voluntary donations should have been better matched by an increase in Lottery grants. And now much more of the funding provided by the Charities board is unthemed and on a continuous basis, so charities needing to finance a project can generally apply at any time.

A good way to give to charity?

Clearly, pound for pound, more of your money reaches charity if you give direct rather than through buying Lottery tickets. Moreover, if you give direct, you can choose which charities you want to give to. With the National Lottery, the relevant body responsible for allocating the funds makes that decision. Evidence from the NCVO suggests that the Lottery is damaging the financial position of some charities – its research estimated that donations fell by 7.2 per cent in 1996 through the public switching to the purchase of Lottery tickets. Evidence from elsewhere suggests that the impact of the Lottery on the charity sector as a whole is less clear. On balance, it seems that the Lottery should be taken simply at face value – a game, a gamble which millions of people find fun, but not an efficient way of giving to charity. If your concern is to support good causes, do not look on the National Lottery as a substitute for giving direct.

Table 4.3 Attitudes towards the National Lottery

	Percentage of people holding this view:		
	The Lottery is a good way to enjoy a flutter for the fun of it	The Lottery is a good way of helping charity	The Lottery is a good way of helping sports and the arts
Whole sample	69%	55%	60%
People playing the Lottery and not giving to charity	78%	59%	61%
People playing the Lottery and giving to charity	81%	62%	69%
People who give to charity but do not play the Lottery	51%	45%	52%
People neither giving to charity nor playing the Lottery	50%	46%	48%

Source: National Council for Voluntary Organisations, *Charitable Giving in Great Britain 1996*, NCVO, 1997

Chapter 5

Other ways of giving to charity

PAY NOW, GIVE LATER

Mary stood chatting to her neighbour, Jack, about charity appeals. 'I set aside a certain amount for charities,' he said, 'but I bide my time about which charities I give to. You see, I have a special charity account – I pay money in, the account claims a bit extra from the taxman, and I have a sort of debit card and cheque book. When I want to donate to a cause, I simply give my card number or write out a cheque drawn on my account.'

'What a splendid idea,' Mary commented. 'Who runs this charity account?'

Apart from the special schemes outlined in Chapter 3, there are a number of other ways of giving to charity that can give either you or the charity some tax advantage. Some are sophisticated schemes, really only suitable if you have a large sum to give. Others are widely useful and can provide a way round some of the inconveniences of the special schemes described in Chapter 3.

There is also one popular method of giving which, though not tax-efficient, does enable the charity to receive more than you give. The various methods are described below.

Giving things rather than cash

You do not have to give just cash as a charitable donation. You could instead give something you own: for example, land, premises, a car, furniture or investments such as shares. As described in Part 2, normally you might have to pay capital gains tax (CGT) and even inheritance tax (IHT) when you give something away. But gifts to charities are generally completely free of these taxes.

For the exemption from IHT to apply, you must relinquish all your rights to whatever it is that you are giving. For example, there might well be a tax bill if you gave the freehold of your home to a charity but continued to live there. For more details about the way CGT and IHT work, see Chapters 6–8.

The government was, at the time of writing, reviewing the way charities are taxed and the tax reliefs available on donations. It has considered whether there should also be income tax relief on gifts of things to charities, but decided that valuing the gifts would be very difficult and open to abuse.

Charitable bequests

If you leave money or assets to charity in your will, your estate pays no IHT on the gift. (Your estate is all your possessions less any debts at the time of death.)

A bequest to charity can also save IHT in a second way, because the value of your estate is reduced by the amount of your gift to charity. This can mean less IHT on the estate as a whole. Bear in mind, though, that making a bequest to charity cuts down the amount of the estate left for your survivors to inherit, so you should not use this as a tax-saving method unless you intended to make philanthropic gifts anyway.

All gifts from your estate when you die – whether to charity or to other organisations or to people – are free of CGT.

A solicitor or your chosen charity can help you to insert an appropriate clause in your will to leave a bequest to charity. See Part 3 for more information about gifts made at the time of death.

CAF Charity Account

The CAF★ is a charity whose aim is to promote charities generally and give them support and assistance. One of the services it runs is the CAF Charity Account. This is a little like a bank account but its sole purpose is for making gifts to charity. The advantages of the Account are that the money you give is increased by tax relief, and you have a convenient, flexible way of giving to a wide range of charities. CAF makes a small charge for running the Account. It works as follows.

You pay money into your Charity Account using a deed of covenant, Gift Aid, or the CAF Payroll Giving scheme called 'Give As You Earn' (see Chapter 3). Because CAF is itself a charity, it is able to claim tax relief on the money you pay in using covenants or Gift Aid and it adds this to your Account. With Payroll Giving you qualify for tax relief directly as normal. When you want to make a gift to a charity, you instruct CAF to transfer money from your Account to the charity. You can do this in several ways, as follows:

- you have a CharityCard which works like a debit card and is especially useful for making donations by phone or post
- CAF provides you with a 'cheque book' of vouchers. You fill in a voucher (for any amount – there is no minimum) and give it to the charity which is to receive your gift – you can even use a voucher to make a donation through a door-to-door collection. The charity sends the voucher to CAF which then transfers the money as you have instructed
- you can ask CAF to make regular payments to a particular charity using a standing order system (a minimum sum of £10 per month is recommended)
- you can ask CAF to make a single payment to a particular charity
- you can leave instructions with CAF about how the money in the account is to be donated in the event of your death
- you can also use your account to pay for Charity Gift Vouchers. Give these to someone who can then use them to make a donation to a charity of their choice.

A further advantage of the Charity Account is that, before carrying out your instructions, CAF automatically runs a check to make sure that the body to which you want to make a payment does indeed have charitable status.

The normal rules which apply to covenants, Gift Aid and Payroll Giving apply when you are using the CAF Charity Account. For example, if you pay into the Account using Gift Aid, you cannot use it to pay subscriptions for membership of charitable bodies. But, if you pay into the Account using a covenant, you can use it to pay your subscription to a few organisations, such as the National Trust (see page

31). The CAF Charity Account is not suitable for non-taxpayers or lower-rate taxpayers who would receive a bill from the Inland Revenue for the tax relief paid over to CAF under covenants or Gift Aid.

For details about the Charity Account, contact CAF at the address at the back of the book.

EXAMPLE 5.1

Jack puts money into his CAF Charity Account using a deed of covenant (see page 28). Under the deed, he pays an after-tax amount of £150 a year into the Account. When each payment is made, CAF reclaims basic-rate tax relief of £44.81 (at 1999–2000 tax rates), bringing the total which is paid into the Account each year to £194.81. (Jack is a basic-rate taxpayer, so he cannot directly reclaim any tax himself.)

CAF deducts a charge of £9.74 a year, leaving £185.07. Out of this, Jack has a standing order to pay £50 a year to the Royal National Institute for Deaf People. He uses his CharityCard and 'cheque book' to make other donations: for example, last year he made out 'cheques' to Help the Aged and the Royal Society for the Prevention of Cruelty to Animals (RSPCA) and used the card to make a phone donation to ChildLine.

Discretionary trusts

A trust is a special legal arrangement where money, shares, or other property are held for the benefit of others. Trustees have the duty of seeing that the property in the trust and any income and gains from it (which together make up the 'trust fund') are used as set out in the trust deed and rules. With a 'discretionary trust', the trustees are given the power to decide how the trust fund is used (within any constraints imposed by the trust rules).

Special tax rules apply to trusts (see Chapter 10), but it is worth noting here that gifts to charity from a discretionary trust can be very tax-efficient. The charity will be able to reclaim all the income tax – usually at 34 per cent (in 1999–2000) rather than just the basic rate – that the trust has paid on the income it gives. If the trust makes a gift to charity of capital, there will be no CGT or IHT to pay on it.

Charitable trusts

Many charities are organised as 'charitable trusts': that is, trustees hold money for the benefit of others and use or distribute it according to the rules set out in the trust deed and rules, but the trust also qualifies for special tax treatment because it meets the requirements for charitable status (see Chapter 2). It is not just organisations that can use charitable trusts; you can, in effect, set up your own charity to give funds to other charities. This would be worth doing if:

- you wanted to give a large sum to charity or to give regular sizeable amounts
- you wanted to split the donation between different charities (especially where each gift is below £250 and so would not qualify for tax relief through Gift Aid) and/or
- you had not yet decided which charities to give some or all of the money to.

Using your own charitable trust is worthwhile only if you want to give a large sum to charity – at least £10,000, say. It can be used to make gifts both during your lifetime and to continue your donations after your death, possibly with the addition of further funds under the terms of your will.

Setting up a charitable trust yourself is a complicated and costly business and you'll need the help of a solicitor. Typically, you would set up a trust – usually a discretionary trust (see Chapter 10 for more about these) – often with yourself as one of the trustees. Once the trust deed has been drawn up (but before it is completed), you need to send it to the Charity Commission,* which, in consultation with the Inland Revenue, will decide whether the trust will qualify as a charity. As long as it will, you can go ahead and set up the trust, and it will be exempt from most taxes in the same way as a normal charity (see Chapter 3). This means that you will be able to make tax-efficient donations into the trust to be passed on to the charities you choose. For example, you could covenant to pay a given sum to the trust for a period of four years or more, or you could donate a lump sum of £250 or more under the Gift Aid scheme. The trust would be able to claim back tax on the payments in the same way as a normal charity. But when the trust itself makes payments to a charity, it cannot use a special scheme, such as a deed of covenant or Gift Aid – you cannot get tax relief twice!

Fortunately, there is a simpler way to set up a charitable trust. CAF★ can set up your own trust for you without any setting up fees or legal costs, just an annual administration fee (1 per cent of funds up to £40,000). Your money (usually a minimum of £10,000) is paid into a CAF investment fund. You can choose between funds focusing on income, growth or deposits. CAF provides the trustees and, since CAF is itself a registered charity, there are no formalities to complete with the Charity Commissioners. You can add to your trust at any time. Income earned by your trust fund is paid into an account where it can be paid out to charities either by standing order or by writing out cheques. CAF provides you with regular income statements and an annual capital statement showing your fund's investments.

EXAMPLE 5.2

Daisy married a wealthy landowner but was widowed many years ago. Daisy's 'good causes' are famous in her family. One of her projects is a charitable trust to which she pays £10,000 a year under a deed of covenant. This is a net covenant, so the £10,000 she pays into the trust is treated as a gift from which tax relief at the basic rate has already been deducted. The charitable trust can claim back that relief which, at the 1999–2000 rate of 23 per cent, comes to £10,000 x 0.23/0.77 = £2,987. So the trust receives £12,987 in total.

Daisy has received basic-rate relief on her donation but she can claim extra relief because she is a higher-rate taxpayer. The gross donation was £12,987. Higher-rate tax relief at 40 per cent less the basic-rate relief already given comes to £12,987 x 40% − £2,987 = £2,208. So the charitable trust has received £12,987 at a cost to Daisy of just £10,000 − £2,208 − £7,792.

The trust is a discretionary trust. Daisy is a trustee and largely decides how the trust money will be used. The trust aims to help people who are in sudden and urgent need: for example, in 1999 it paid £5,000 to charities providing famine relief in Africa, £1,500 to help Kosovan refugees, and £1,500 to a local charity to help families in financial distress following the closure of a major employer in the area. If the trust does not pay out the full amount covenanted in any year, the remainder is invested to be used for charitable causes in future years.

You can set up a charitable trust in your will to receive a bequest. The bequest would reduce the size of your estate for tax purposes and could mean there is less IHT to be paid (see Part 3). The deed and rules of the charitable trust would specify how the bequest is to be used: for example, you might want the capital to remain invested while the income from it is donated to charity, or you might want the trustees to decide to which charities the capital and/or income are to be given. You can even set up a 'temporary charitable trust' where the trust funds are used for charitable purposes for a specified period but then revert to a non-charitable use: for example, you might direct that income be donated to charity until your grandchildren come of age when the trust money is to be split between them. When a temporary charitable trust stops being used for charitable purposes, there will be an income tax bill and possibly a CGT bill. The rules are complex, so seek professional advice before setting up this type of trust.

There is always a risk that a trust set up under a will might not be recognised by the authorities as charitable even though it was your intention that it should be. To avoid this risk, you could set up the trust during your lifetime, paying just a small amount into it now; this gives you the chance to alter the trust if the Inland Revenue is not satisfied that it meets the requirements for a charity. Once charitable status has been secured, you can safely make a bequest to the trust in your will.

Gifts from businesses

If you run your own company or you are self-employed, there are a number of tax-efficient ways in which you can give to charity. Similarly, a club which is set up as a limited company can use the methods outlined in this section.

Ideally, you would be able to treat a gift to charity as an allowable business expense since this would reduce your profits and thus tax on them. But normal business rules apply and your gift would have to be made 'wholly and exclusively for the purposes of trade' in order to be allowable. Most charitable gifts just do not fit the bill. However, a number of quirks and concessions in the tax rules mean that you should be able to treat the following sorts of gifts to charities as an allowable expense:

- small gifts of money, or gifts in kind, to support a local charity provided the gift has a business purpose – for example, donations to a local charity that benefits your employees in some way
- sponsorship of a charity event as long as it provides you with advertising
- all the costs of employing someone, even though seconded temporarily to work for a charity rather than working for you.

Most business gifts to charity are *not* allowable expenses, but businesses can use both deeds of covenant (see page 28) and Gift Aid (see page 34) – including Millennium Gift Aid (see page 37) – to make gifts in much the same way as an individual. The business makes a gift from which basic-rate income tax has been deducted. The charity reclaims the tax from the Inland Revenue, thus boosting the size of the gift. If you are self-employed, you simply keep the tax you have deducted from the gift as long as you are liable for at least that much tax yourself. A company must pay the tax it has deducted from the gift over to the Inland Revenue, but can then deduct the gross amount of the gift from its taxable profits and thus get relief from corporation tax.

It is worth noting that, under a covenant, you do not have to specify that each payment you make will be a particular sum of money. You could instead covenant, say, a specified proportion of your annual profits.

EXAMPLE 5.3

Jack is the treasurer of a car racing club which meets regularly during the summer months. At the meetings, both members and spectators are charged an entrance fee and there are other takings for refreshments. The club always gives the income from these meetings, after deducting costs, to a charity.

The club is set up as a limited company. In order to take advantage of the tax relief available on charitable giving, it decides to covenant the profits from each season's race meetings to the Cancer and Leukaemia in Childhood charity (CLIC). Despite the fact that the profits vary and cannot be known at the time the covenant is drawn up, this is a valid form of covenant.

At present, traders who donate used equipment (e.g. redundant computers) or their own stock to schools and colleges do not have to account for any tax on these items. In the March 1998 Budget, the same tax treatment was extended to traders who give similar support to educational projects in the countries eligible for Millennium Gift Aid. And, as part of its review of charity taxation, the government has announced that as part of the 1999 Budget measures this tax treatment will be opened up to cover all such gifts to any charitable cause.

Donation cards

A number of charities and credit card companies have combined forces to issue donation cards (also called 'affinity cards'). These are normal credit cards, but the card company promises to make donations to charity (or sometimes non-charitable bodies, such as football clubs and political parties) linked to your use of the credit card. For example, if you take out a Midland Bank National Trust Visa card, the bank donates £10 to the Trust at the time you open the card account and donates a further 5p each time you make a transaction through the card. Co-operative Bank offers a range of donation cards linked to Help the Aged, Oxfam, Save the Children and the Royal Society for the Protection of Birds (RSPB) among other bodies (some charitable, some not). With all these, the Co-operative Bank gives £5 or £10 to the organisation when you first take out the card and donates further sums equal to 0.25 per cent of the value of the transactions made using the card. Bank of Scotland and MBNA are two of the largest donation card issuers, with cards linked to over 500 and 650 organisations, respectively.

The credit card company can use a donation card scheme to make tax-efficient donations to charity, but it is, of course, a marketing exercise for the company, attracting customers and helping to project a caring image. If you use a credit card anyway, a donation card is a way in which you can play an indirect role in giving to charity, but compare interest rates and other terms with standard credit cards before you commit yourself. It may be better to choose a low-cost ordinary card and arrange to make your donations direct to charity. If you do not normally use a credit card, you should be wary of taking out a donation card: do not run up debts that you cannot afford.

Summary of gifts to charity

Method of giving	Can you give a single lump sum?	Suitable for 'small' gifts (i.e. less than £250)?	Can a payment be split into gifts for several charities?
Covenant	No	Yes	No
Loan covenant	Yes	Yes[20]	No
Gift Aid	Yes	No	No
Millennium Gift Aid	Yes	Yes	No
Payroll Giving	No	Yes	Yes
Give an asset	Yes	Yes	No
Charitable bequest	Yes	Yes	Maybe
CAF Charity Account – by covenant	No	Yes	Yes
CAF Charity Account – by Gift Aid	Yes	No	Yes
CAF Charity Account – by Payroll Giving	No	Yes	Yes
Discretionary trust	Yes	No[21]	Yes
Charitable trust	Yes	No[21]	Yes

[20] But administration costs mean that for gifts under £100 or so it would not normally be worthwhile using this method.

[21] Small gifts are technically possible but unsuitable, given the cost and administration involved in setting up the trust.

Part 2

Lifetime gifts to

family and friends

Chapter 6

Tax-free gifts

THE CHOICE OF GIFT MATTERS

'Sylvia,' Jeffrey turned solemnly to his wife, 'I think we should give Tom a helping hand to buy a home now that he's settling down.'

'I couldn't agree more. But to be fair to the girls, we ought to set aside some money to help them later on too,' replied Sylvia.

'It doesn't have to be money, of course – they might like to have one or two of those paintings my mother left me. I wonder if it makes a tax difference? I do believe that we could give Tom a bit of money as a wedding present without running into tax problems . . .'

You need to be aware of two main taxes when making a gift to someone: capital gains tax (CGT) and inheritance tax (IHT). Some gifts can also affect your income tax position – an aspect which can be to your advantage as long as you arrange the gift in a suitable way (see Chapter 9). This chapter looks at gifts you can make during your lifetime that are either free of CGT, free of IHT, or completely free of both taxes. Subsequent chapters look at gifts which may be taxable.

Capital gains tax

When you give someone something that you own, you are treated for tax purposes as making a 'disposal' of an 'asset'. An 'asset' is simply something you own. 'Disposal' means ceasing to own the asset, however this comes about – the tax position when you give away an asset is essentially the same as if you had sold it.

If an asset's value at the time you give it away is greater than its value at the time you first started to own it, there *could* be a CGT bill. But don't panic! Often, you won't have to pay any CGT, because:

- some assets are outside the scope of CGT
- gains from some transactions are always tax-free.

The scope of capital gains tax

CGT is a tax on the disposal of *assets*. 'Assets' covers virtually all types of possessions: land, buildings (including your home), stocks and shares, paintings, furniture, patents and copyrights, debts owed to you, and so on. 'Assets', for CGT purposes, does not include sterling currency – so a gift of money cannot result in a CGT bill. By an interesting quirk of the law, sovereigns minted after 1837 still count as sterling currency and are therefore outside the CGT net. (Sovereigns minted before then count as 'chattels' – see below.)

Certain other assets are specifically exempt from CGT. These are looked at in the following sections.

'Chattels'

These are tangible, movable assets – basically your personal belongings, such as clothes, books, compact discs and so on, and your household goods. An item in this category is exempt from CGT provided it has a predicted useful life of 50 years or less and you have not used it in a business.

For chattels with an expected life of more than 50 years, any gain is exempt if the value of the item at the time you dispose of it is no more than £6,000. If a chattel's value is more than £6,000, any gain can be worked out in a special way which may reduce the CGT bill (see Example 7.3 on page 77). There are rules to prevent you reducing the CGT payable by splitting up a set – for example, a set of chairs – and then giving all the parts of the set to the same person.

If you give away or sell a decoration awarded (e.g. to you or a relative) for valour or gallantry, there is no CGT on any gain, unless you had originally bought the decoration or exchanged something of value for it.

Your home

There is no CGT to pay when you dispose of part or all of your only, or main, home. This exemption includes your garden up to a reasonable size (usually half a hectare – just over an acre – but it can be more if the style and size of house warrants a larger garden).

If you have more than one home, you will have to nominate one as your main home for CGT purposes. A husband and wife who live together can have only one main home between them. (But if one of them counts as non-resident for a tax year, husband and wife can each have a main home for CGT purposes.)

You may lose part of the exemption if part of your home was set aside exclusively for business. There may also be a CGT bill when you dispose of your home, if you have lived away for long periods. For more details, see Chapter 15.

EXAMPLE 6.1

Daisy has decided that Hadley Hall where she has lived since her marriage is now too large for her needs. She plans to give the Hall to her only son, Albert, and buy a cottage nearby. When Daisy inherited the Hall on her husband's death it was worth £150,000. It is now worth twice that, but there will be no CGT bill because:

- the Hall is Daisy's only home, and
- although the garden runs to over two acres, the Inland Revenue has agreed that this is in keeping with the house.

However, Daisy does need to consider her position with regard to inheritance tax (see Chapter 8).

Motor vehicles

There is no CGT on gains from selling or giving away a private car (including vintage or classic cars), a motorbike, or other private motor vehicle. This exemption can also apply to a vehicle used for business provided it was 'commonly used as a private vehicle'. However, the exemption does not stretch to vehicles that are not commonly used as private vehicles and are unsuitable for use in that way – so watch out if you're tempted by surplus Ministry of Defence tanks or similar exotica!

Foreign currency

There is no CGT on gains from buying and selling foreign money which you have obtained for your own use – for a holiday abroad, say, or for buying or running a holiday home abroad, or for use during a business trip.

Some investments

Gains on some investments are completely free from CGT: for example, National Savings investments, Premium Bonds, British government stocks (commonly known as gilt-edged stock or gilts), many corporate bonds, and shares held through a Personal Equity Plan (PEP) or Individual Savings Account (ISA). Provided certain conditions are met, gains on shares bought through a Business Expansion Scheme (BES) and its successor, the Enterprise Investment Scheme (EIS) are also CGT-free. Similarly, gains on investments in Venture Capital Trusts (VCTs) are also free of CGT provided you invest for five years or more.

Insurance policies

Payment from a life insurance policy, whether on maturity, early surrender, or even through selling the policy to someone else, is usually exempt from CGT. The exemption does not apply, however, if you bought the policy from someone else, for example, through an auction.

Your rights to certain payments

If you dispose of your right to receive an income under an annuity or a covenant, say, there is usually no CGT on any gain you make as a result. Similarly, if you give away your right to benefit under the terms of a trust or your right to repayment of money you have lent someone, there is usually no CGT – but there could be, if in the first place you had bought these rights.

Tax-free transactions

Some *transactions* are also exempt from CGT. This means that the following types of gift are free of CGT.

Gifts between husband and wife
Gifts between husband and wife are free of CGT provided the couple are living together.

Gifts to charities and certain other bodies
Donations and gifts to charity, and to various other institutions, including many museums and art galleries, local authorities, government departments and universities, are CGT-free.

Gifts for the public benefit
Gifts of 'eligible property' to any non-profit body approved by the government are outside the CGT net. 'Eligible property' includes land or buildings of outstanding historic or aesthetic interest, and property to be used as a source of income for the upkeep of such land or buildings. It also covers items such as books, pictures, scientific collections and so on which are judged to be of national interest.

Gifts if you move abroad
Since 17 March 1998, if you leave the UK to take up residence abroad, you can give away assets you acquired while still in the UK without paying any CGT, but only if you are resident abroad for at least five years (see page 149).

Gifts on death
When you die, you are deemed to make a gift of all you then own to your heirs, but whatever, and however much, you leave, it is always free of CGT.

Inheritance tax

IHT is a tax on the 'transfer of value' from one person to another. 'Transfer of value' means a gift (or other transaction) which reduces the value of the possessions (the 'estate') owned by the person making the transfer. In theory, it could apply to any gift but, as with CGT, there are exemptions and adjustments. This means that on most lifetime gifts there is no IHT to pay, because:

- various types of gift are always free of IHT

- some gifts, called 'potentially exempt transfers', are free of tax, provided the giver lives on for seven years after making the gift (see page 68).

Gifts which are always free of IHT

The scope of IHT is, on the face of it, wider than that of CGT because IHT covers all assets – including money, as well as houses, land, pictures, furniture, and so on. Gifts made in certain circumstances or between certain people or bodies are also free of IHT. This applies to the following gifts, whether you make them during your lifetime or as bequests in your will (see Chapter 12).

Gifts between husband and wife

Gifts between husband and wife up to any amount are tax-free as long as the couple are not divorced. Even a husband and wife who are separated benefit from this exemption. If the husband or wife receiving the gift is not 'domiciled' in the UK, the exemption is limited to a total of £55,000. (Your place of 'domicile' is, broadly, where you make your permanent home and intend to end your days.)

Gifts to charities and certain other bodies

This exemption from IHT is similar to the equivalent one for CGT (see page 63). It covers outright donations and gifts of any amount to UK charities, national museums and art galleries, universities, local authorities, government departments, and a number of other bodies.

Gifts for the public benefit

Again this is similar to the associated CGT exemption. Gifts of land, buildings, works of art, and so on, of outstanding national interest are free of IHT if given to a suitable non-profit-making body that has been approved by the government.

Gifts to political parties

A gift to a political party is exempt from IHT, provided the party has at least two MPs or polled at least 150,000 votes at the most recent general election.

Housing Associations

Gifts of land to a Registered Housing Association are exempt.

Lifetime gifts which are free of IHT

The following gifts are free of IHT only when they are made during your lifetime (i.e. not in your will).

Normal expenditure out of income

If you can show that a gift you are making is one of a regular pattern of similar gifts and that you are making it out of your income (rather than from your savings or other capital), the gift will be exempt from IHT.

Gifts made under a legally binding agreement, such as a deed of covenant, will usually be treated as regular gifts. So too will premiums you pay for an insurance policy that is for the benefit of someone else: for example, a policy on your life which would pay out to your children in the event of your death. If the gifts are not made under any formal agreement but you intend that they will be regular gifts, they can still qualify for the exemption. The first gift or two might not be treated as exempt at the time you make them but, once a regular pattern has been established, they can be reassessed as tax-exempt.

The gifts must be made out of your income, so you need to be able to show that you have enough income left to meet your day-to-day living expenses. The income can be from any source – a job, interest from investments, and so on. But bear in mind that the capital element of a 'purchased life annuity' (see Glossary) is not income, nor are withdrawals from 'single-premium life insurance bonds' (see Glossary).

Normally, the gifts would be cash. If you make gifts which are not cash you will have to be able to prove that the things you are giving were bought out of your income.

Gifts for the maintenance of your family

Money or things which you give to provide housing, food, education, or some other form of maintenance, for your husband or wife, ex-husband or ex-wife, children or a dependent relative are outside the IHT net.

As far as husband and wife are concerned, the normal exemption for gifts between married couples (see opposite) would usually apply rather than this exemption. But if either husband or wife are 'domiciled' (see page 64) abroad, this exemption could be useful. This exemption will usually cover maintenance agreements made as a result of a marriage breakdown.

The definition of children is very wide, covering stepchildren, illegitimate children, and adopted children, but it does not extend to grandchildren. Usually a child is considered to be adult when he or she reaches the age of 18 but, if he or she goes on to full-time education or training after that age, the IHT exemption can carry on.

A 'dependent relative' can be any relative of you or your husband or wife who is unable to maintain him or herself because of old age or infirmity. It also includes your mother or mother-in-law, even if not elderly or infirm, if they are widowed, separated or divorced. As a concession, this exemption is also extended to gifts to your mother if she is unmarried, provided she is financially dependent on you.

Yearly tax-free exemption

Every tax year, you can give away £3,000-worth of gifts without their counting in any way for IHT purposes. This exemption is in addition to the other exemptions, so a gift which qualifies for some other exemption does not count towards the £3,000 annual limit.

If you do not use up the full exemption one year, you can carry it forward to the next year – but not to any subsequent year. This means that, if you used none of last year's exemption, you could make up to £6,000 worth of gifts this year that qualify for the exemption. Gifts always use up the exemption for the tax year in which they are made first *before* using up any carried-foward exemption.

EXAMPLE 6.2

Albert is not altogether pleased at being given Hadley Hall by Daisy (see page 61). She has paid little attention to the house in the last 20 years and now the roof needs re-slating and all the exterior woodwork is in dire need of a new coat of paint. After several heated discussions, Daisy finally agrees to give Albert £5,000 towards the cost of the work. Albert persuades Daisy to pay the money to a company which he runs rather than direct to him.

A gift from a person to a company would usually be taxable under the IHT rules. But, in this case, there is no IHT to pay because Daisy has not used her annual exemption for either this year or last year. The gift to Albert uses up the full £3,000 exemption available for this year and £2,000 of the exemption carried forward from last year. There remains £1,000 of last year's exemption which can be set against any other chargeable gifts made this year, but it cannot be carried forward any further.

Small gifts

You can make as many gifts as you like of up to £250 to each person, and these will be exempt. You cannot combine the small gift exemption with another exemption to give more than £250 to *one* person, but you can, say, give £3,000 to one recipient and gifts of £250 to any number of *other* people.

This exemption will generally cover birthday and Christmas presents, and any other small gifts you make during the year.

Wedding gifts

As a parent, you can give up to £5,000 to the happy couple free of IHT. A grandparent (or other ancestor) can give up to £2,500. Anyone else can give up to £1,000. The bride and groom can give up to £2,500 to each other, but this limit will not be relevant if both are 'domiciled' (see page 64) in the UK, since the exemption for married couples will apply.

The exemptions apply to each giver: for example, assuming both bride's and groom's mothers and fathers were living, the couple could receive a maximum of £20,000 from their parents.

The exemptions under this section can also apply to a marriage settlement which aims to benefit the bride or groom, their children, or the husbands or wives of their children.

Potentially exempt transfers

A potentially exempt transfer (PET) is a gift from a person either to another person or to certain types of trust (see Chapter 10) that is not covered by some other IHT exemption. As long as the person making the gift survives for seven years after the date of the gift, there is no IHT to pay. If the giver dies within seven years, there may be an IHT bill. PETs are looked at in detail in Chapter 8.

EXAMPLE 6.3

Daisy's gift of Hadley Hall to Albert is valued at £300,000. Despite the substantial value of the gift, there is no IHT to pay at the time of the gift, because it counts as a potentially exempt transfer (PET). As long as Daisy survives for seven years, there will be no IHT at all. But if she does die within that time, the gift will be reassessed and tax may then be due, calculated using the value of the Hall at the time of the original gift (i.e. £300,000), Daisy's overall IHT position at that time and IHT rates at the time of death (see page 104).

Combining CGT and IHT exemptions

Some types of gift are specifically exempt from both CGT and IHT: for example, gifts to charities, museums, and so on, and gifts for the public benefit. Other gifts will be completely tax-free as long as they fall within an IHT exemption *and* you give cash or other assets which are not liable for CGT. Chapters 7 and 8 describe other situations in which either CGT or IHT may not be payable. You can make use of the exemptions in these situations too, to ensure that your gifts are free of both taxes.

EXAMPLE 6.4

Jeffrey gives his son, Tom, £4,000 in cash as a wedding gift to help him and his new wife buy a home of their own. There is no CGT on a gift of cash and no IHT on a wedding gift of this size.

Jeffrey also wants to give his youngest daughter, Ruth, a gift of similar value. She decides she would like to have a watercolour – a family heirloom – which is valued at £4,500. This counts as a 'chattel' (see page 60) and, since its value is less than £6,000, there is no CGT liability. The gift is a PET under the IHT rules, and so, since Jeffrey is expected to live a good many years longer, the gift is likely to be completely free of IHT.

Chapter 7

Capital gains tax on lifetime gifts

AND STILL NO TAX TO PAY

'Congratulations!' Frederick raised his glass and drank his son's health. 'And now you are come of age, it's time you had some financial responsibility . . . Happy birthday.'

Frederick handed an envelope to his son. Inside was a certificate for £12,300-worth of unit trusts. 'I don't know what to say, Dad,' gasped Colin in surprise.

'Well, thank-you might be a start. It's not a trivial gift, you know – though at least I didn't have to pay any capital gains tax on it,' Frederick chuckled, with a satisfied smile on his face.

From April 1998 onwards, the way capital gains are taxed has been changed. Indexation allowance (see page 75) has been replaced by taper relief (see page 73). This reduces a taxable gain according to the length of time you have held an asset but there is no longer any distinction between 'gains' purely due to increases in the general price level and 'real' gains in value. Because of the way losses are treated under the new system, they are effectively tapered too and so worth less as a means of offsetting gains – see page 88. And due to oddities of the new system, in some cases where you have offsetting losses, some of your loss relief may be wasted – see page 88.

A knock-on effect of taper relief has been an end to share-pooling – see page 84 – which means extra paperwork for you. And the government took the opportunity also to abolish 'bed-and-breakfasting' – see page 84.

The overall impact of the changes has been to make capital gains tax more onerous than it was under the pre-1998 regime.

However, in the 1999 Budget the government announced that the tax rates applicable to capital gains are being aligned with the rates for savings income. Previously capital gains had been taxed at the same rates as income. The change means that you do not benefit from the new 10 per cent rate of income tax on your gains (introduced from April 1999). On the other hand, if you are a basic-rate taxpayer, your gains are now taxed at just 20 per cent instead of 23 per cent.

No tax to pay?

Chapter 6 looked at gifts that are specifically exempt from capital gains tax (CGT). But even if your gift is not covered by one of the exemptions – for example, if you are giving away shares, a second home or a valuable heirloom – there could still be no tax to pay, because:

- from 6 April 1998 onwards, your gain could have been reduced by taper relief, with the greatest relief given to the assets you have held the longest
- increases in the value of an asset in line with inflation up to April 1998 are not taxed
- you can reduce gains on some assets by deducting losses made on various other assets
- everyone has an 'annual exempt amount' – a tax-free slice of several thousands of pounds of gains which are automatically tax-free each year.

Your first step in working out what tax might be due is to calculate the basic gain on the asset you are giving away. What happens next will depend on when you first acquired the asset and the period over which you have held it.

The basic gain

- Take the 'final value' of the gift. This will usually be the price you would have received if you had sold the asset on the open market.
- Deduct the 'initial value'. This is the price you originally paid for it or its market value at the time you first became the owner.

- Deduct any allowable expenses. These are costs you incurred in acquiring and disposing of the asset (e.g. commission paid to a broker, the cost of an expert valuation or solicitor's fees) and any expenses associated with enhancing the value of the asset (e.g. adding an extension to a property) but not spending on maintenance and repairs.

Assets acquired on or after 1 April 1998

For an asset acquired on or after 1 April 1998, the result of the calculation above is your 'chargeable gain' (if the answer is greater than zero) or your 'allowable loss' (if the answer is less than zero).

Where you have made a chargeable gain, you can deduct any losses you are claiming for the tax year in which the gift is made (see page 88 for more about losses). The resulting figure is your 'net chargeable gain'.

You do not necessarily pay tax on the whole of your net chargeable gain. The government wants to encourage people to hold investments for the longer rather than the shorter term in the belief that this provides a healthier environment for British business. Therefore taper relief reduces the amount of your net chargeable gain with the largest reduction given to the assets you have held for the longest – see Table 7.1. For non-business assets, there is no reduction at all until you have held the asset for three years. The reduction then depends on the number of complete tax years since 5 April 1998 for which you have held the asset. The maximum reduction is given after ten complete years. Taper relief is more generous if the asset you are giving away counts as a business asset (see page 94).

If you make a gift to your husband or wife and he or she subsequently disposes of the asset, taper relief at the time of disposal is counted from the period when you first started to own the asset not from the later date when the gift was made.

Table 7.1 CGT taper relief for non-business assets

If you have held the asset for this many complete tax years after 5 April 1998:	Your net chargeable gain is reduced by this percentage:	Only this percentage of your gain counts as chargeable:	For example, a net chargeable gain of £5,000 is reduced to:
0	No reduction	100%	£5,000
1	No reduction	100%	£5,000
2	No reduction	100%	£5,000
3	5%	95%	£4,750
4	10%	90%	£4,500
5	15%	85%	£4,250
6	20%	80%	£4,000
7	25%	75%	£3,750
8	30%	70%	£3,500
9	35%	65%	£3,250
10 or more	40%	60%	£3,000

EXAMPLE 7.1

Carole bought a holiday cottage in May 1998 for £65,000. The buying costs amounted to £1,800. In August 1998, Carole added a large conservatory to the cottage at a cost of £2,900. In June 2006, Carole gives the cottage to her niece, Becky. It is then valued at £92,000 and the costs incurred in making the transfer to Becky amount to £1,020. Carole is deemed to have made a chargeable gain on the gift as follows:

Final value of the cottage	£92,000
less Initial value	£65,000
less Allowable expenses	£ 2,900
	£ 1,020
Chargeable gain	£23,080
less Allowable losses	£ 0
Net chargeable gain before CGT taper relief	£23,080

Number of complete tax years for which cottage held (6 April 1999 to 5 April 2006)	7 years
Percentage taper	75%
Net chargeable gain after taper relief (75% x £23,080)	£17,310

CGT on gifts of assets acquired before 1 April 1998 but after March 1982

If you give away an asset which you started to own on or after 31 March 1982 but before 1 April 1998, work out the basic gain as on page 72. Divide your period of ownership into two:

- holding period 1: date of acquisition up to April 1998
- holding period 2: 6 April 1998 up to date when gift is made.

Holding period 1: indexation allowance

In respect of holding period 1 (date of acquisition up to April 1998), you can deduct indexation allowance. Take the initial value of the asset (see page 72) and each allowable expense and multiply each of these values by the appropriate indexation factor. Add the result together and the total is the indexation allowance.

The indexation factor for the initial value and each expense is derived from the change in the Retail Prices Index (RPI) since the expense was incurred up to 5 April 1998 (or, if earlier, the date on which the gift was made). This is described on page 80.

The effect of the indexation allowance is to strip out any gains which are simply the result of inflation – i.e. do not represent any real increase in your wealth. However, since 6 April 1995, the indexation allowance can at most wipe out the whole gain – it cannot be used to create or increase a loss for CGT purposes. (Before that date, the indexation allowance could create or increase a loss, although, under transitional rules, such losses were restricted to a maximum of £10,000 in the period 30 November 1993 to 5 April 1995).

Deducting the indexation allowance from your basic gain gives you your 'indexed gain'.

Holding period 2: taper relief

Having found your indexed gain, you next work out how much taper relief you qualify for in respect of holding period 2 (6 April 1998 to date of gift) using the rules described on page 73 with one exception: you are allowed to add one extra year to the holding period for any asset which you already owned on 17 March 1998 (the Budget day on which taper relief was announced).

EXAMPLE 7.2

On his 18th birthday on 1 September 2001, Colin is given a portfolio of unit trusts by his father, Frederick. Frederick originally bought the units in July 1991 for £4,700. They are now worth £12,300. As Frederick is 'disposing' of the units, there could be a CGT bill. To work out whether he has made a chargeable gain, Frederick makes the following calculations:

Basic gain

Final value of units	£12,300
less Initial value	£4,700
less fee paid to investment adviser	
at time units were bought	£150
	£7,450

Indexation allowance

Initial value and allowable expenses	
incurred at time of acquisition	£4,850
Indexation factor (see page 80)	0.215
Indexation allowance for period to	
April 1998 (0.215 x £4,850)	£1,043

Taper relief

Indexed gain (£7,450 − £1,043)	£6,407

less allowable losses	£0
Net chargeable gain before taper relief	£6,407
Number of complete tax years since 5 April 1998 for which asset held	3
Plus one year because asset acquired before 17 March 1998	4
Percentage taper (see page 74)	90%
Net chargeable gain after taper relief (90% x £6,407)	£5,766

Gifts made before 1 April 1998

If you gave away an asset before 1 April 1998, taper relief does not apply at all. Indexation allowance will apply for the whole period you owned the asset from 31 March onwards. The allowance is given as described on page 75 but calculated only up to the date of the gift (rather than to April 1998). For details about calculating the indexation allowance, see page 80.

EXAMPLE 7.3

In February 1999 Sylvia and Jeffrey decided to give their elder daughter, Hazel, an oil painting she had asked for. It has been in Jeffrey's family for several generations and in February was valued at £7,000.

The gift counts as a disposal of a 'chattel' with a predicted life of more than 50 years. Its value is greater than £6,000, so there may be a CGT bill (see page 60), but special rules apply in calculating the chargeable gain: the gain will be the *lower* of either five-thirds of the excess of the disposal value over £6,000 or the gain (before deducting any losses or taper relief but after deducting any indexation allowance) worked out in the normal way.

When Jeffrey inherited the painting in 1987, it was valued at £3,500. Jeffrey can claim an indexation allowance (see page 80) of £2,170. For simplicity, assume there are no allowable expenses. The two calculations are as follows:

Method 1

Final value	£7,000
less £6,000	£6,000
	£1,000
5/3 x £1,000	£1,667

Method 2

Final value	£7,000
less initial value	£3,500
less indexation allowance	£2,170
	£1,330

Method 2 gives the lowest answer, so Jeffrey's chargeable gain is £1,330.

CGT on gifts of assets acquired before April 1982

Gains due to inflation were not always tax-free. The legislation taking them out of the CGT net is effective only from the end of March 1982 onwards. For an asset which you started to own *before* 1 April 1982 (or 6 April 1982 in the case of shares), the sums are slightly different from those outlined in the previous section. There are two methods of calculating your chargeable gain, as follows:

- *Method 1* The initial value is usually taken to be the value of the asset on 31 March 1982, and the indexation allowance for the initial cost is based on inflation since that date. Any allowable expenses incurred before 31 March 1982 are ignored; allowable expenses after that date are indexed in the normal way.
- *Method 2* If working out your chargeable gain using Method 1 would result in a higher CGT bill than taking into account the full period during which you have owned the asset up to April 1998, you can instead work out the chargeable gain based on the whole period. In this case, the initial value is the actual value at the time you first acquired the asset. The indexation allowance is worked out based on either the initial value *or* the asset's value on 31 March 1982 but adjusting for inflation only since March 1982.

If Method 1 and Method 2 both result in a gain, your chargeable gain will be the lower of the two amounts. If both methods give a loss, your allowable loss is the smaller amount. If one gives a gain and the other a loss, you are deemed to have made neither a gain nor a loss – there will be no CGT to pay but no loss to offset against gains on other assets. If Method 2 would, in any case, have produced neither a gain nor a loss, that method is used whatever the result of using Method 1 would have been. The comparison of the outcomes of Methods 1 and 2 is called the 'Kink test'.

You can choose to use just Method 1. If you do, *all* your assets will be covered by the election. The effect is as if you had sold all your assets on 31 March 1982 and immediately rebought them. It will usually be worth making this choice if the values of all or most of your assets were higher on 31 March 1982 than they were at the time you first acquired them.

EXAMPLE 7.4

Tom's grandmother, Emily, gives Tom some shares as a wedding present in June 1999. She originally bought them in 1979 for £1,500 and they are now worth £11,000. On 31 March 1982, they were valued at just £1,000. Emily's chargeable gain is worked out using Methods 1 and 2 as follows:

Method 1

Final value of shares	£11,000
less value of shares on 31 March 1982	£1,000
less indexation allowance for period March 1982 to April 1998 (see below)	£1,047
Chargeable gain (before losses and taper relief)	£8,953

Method 2

Final value of shares	£11,000
less initial value of shares	£1,500
less indexation allowance	£1,571
Chargeable gain (before losses and taper relief)	£7,929

Indexation allowance

Indexation factor for inflation from 31 March 1982 to April 1998	1.047
Indexation allowance using value at 31 March 1982 (1.047 x £1,000)	£1,047
Indexation allowance using initial value (1.047 x £1,500)	£1,571

The result is smaller using Method 2, therefore Emily's net chargeable gain is £7,929.

Working out your indexation allowance

Your indexation allowance is the appropriate indexation factor multiplied by the relevant initial value or allowable expense. The indexation factor depends on the month when you first acquired the asset or incurred the expense. Until April 1998, the factor also varied according to the month in which you disposed of the asset. But, since indexation allowance now runs only up to April 1998, there is just one set of indexation factors which applies to all disposals you make from April 1998 onwards. These are shown in Table 7.2. Look along the left-hand side to find the year in which you acquired the asset or incurred the expense; run your eye across to the column for the relevant month. This is the indexation factor you should use. See Example 7.5.

EXAMPLE 7.5

In September 1999, Christina gives her daughter Michelle some jewellery which Christina inherited from her own mother in February 1990. She needs to work out what indexation allowance she can claim for the period February 1990 to April 1998. Using Table 7.2, she finds the year 1990 along the left-hand side and runs across to the column for February. The entry tells her that the indexation factor to use is 0.353.

Table 7.2 Indexation factors for gifts or disposals you make from April 1998 onwards

	Jan	Feb	Mar	April	May	June	July	Aug	Sept	Oct	Nov	Dec
1982	–	–	1.047	1.006	0.992	0.987	0.986	0.985	0.987	0.977	0.967	0.971
1983	0.968	0.960	0.956	0.929	0.921	0.917	0.906	0.898	0.889	0.883	0.876	0.871
1984	0.872	0.865	0.859	0.834	0.828	0.823	0.825	0.808	0.804	0.793	0.788	0.789
1985	0.783	0.769	0.752	0.716	0.708	0.704	0.707	0.703	0.704	0.701	0.695	0.693
1986	0.689	0.683	0.681	0.665	0.662	0.663	0.667	0.662	0.654	0.652	0.638	0.632
1987	0.626	0.620	0.616	0.597	0.596	0.596	0.597	0.593	0.588	0.580	0.573	0.574
1988	0.574	0.568	0.562	0.537	0.531	0.525	0.524	0.507	0.500	0.485	0.478	0.474
1989	0.465	0.454	0.448	0.423	0.414	0.409	0.408	0.404	0.395	0.384	0.372	0.369
1990	0.361	0.353	0.339	0.300	0.288	0.283	0.282	0.269	0.258	0.248	0.251	0.252
1991	0.249	0.242	0.237	0.222	0.218	0.213	0.215	0.213	0.208	0.204	0.199	0.198
1992	0.199	0.193	0.189	0.171	0.167	0.167	0.171	0.171	0.166	0.162	0.164	0.168
1993	0.179	0.171	0.167	0.156	0.152	0.153	0.156	0.151	0.146	0.147	0.148	0.146
1994	0.151	0.144	0.141	0.128	0.124	0.124	0.129	0.124	0.121	0.120	0.119	0.114
1995	0.114	0.107	0.102	0.091	0.087	0.085	0.091	0.085	0.080	0.085	0.085	0.079
1996	0.083	0.078	0.073	0.066	0.063	0.063	0.067	0.062	0.057	0.057	0.057	0.053
1997	0.053	0.049	0.046	0.040	0.036	0.032	0.032	0.026	0.021	0.019	0.019	0.016
1998	0.019	0.014	0.011	–	–	–	–	–	–	–	–	–

If you need the indexation factor for a disposal made before April 1998, you can work it out from the Retail Prices Index (RPI). This index is the most commonly used measure of the level of prices in the UK. Table 7.3 lists the RPI from March 1982 up to April 1998. The latest RPI figure you will need for CGT calculations is that for April 1998.

To work out the appropriate indexation factor, take the RPI figure for the month in which you disposed of the asset – call this R_D – and the RPI figure for the month in which you acquired the asset (or incurred the expense), or for March 1982, whichever is appropriate – call this R_I. Then make the following calculation:

$$\text{Indexation factor} = \frac{R_D - R_I}{R_I}$$

Indexation factors are rounded to the nearest third decimal place. See also page 75 for rules on indexation allowances and losses if you gave away assets during the period 30 November 1993 to 5 April 1995.

EXAMPLE 7.6

Jack gave his mother, Rachel, some shares in February 1998. He originally bought them in August 1981, but he can claim indexation allowance only since March 1982. To work out the allowance, he takes the RPI for February 1998 which is 160.3 (see Table 7.3 opposite) and the RPI for March 1982 which is 79.44. He does the following sum:

$$\text{Indexation factor} = \frac{R_D - R_I}{R_I} \quad \frac{160.3 - 79.44}{79.44}$$
$$= 1.018$$

The indexation factor Jack needs to use is 1.018. The indexation allowance he can claim is the factor multiplied by the relevant initial value or allowable expense.

Table 7.3   Retail Prices Index (Base: January 1987 = 100)

	Jan	Feb	Mar	April	May	June	July	Aug	Sept	Oct	Nov	Dec
1982	–	–	79.44	81.04	81.62	81.85	81.88	81.90	81.85	82.26	82.66	82.51
1983	82.61	82.97	83.12	84.28	84.64	84.84	85.30	85.68	86.06	86.36	86.67	86.89
1984	86.84	87.20	87.48	88.64	88.97	89.20	89.10	89.94	90.11	90.67	90.95	90.87
1985	91.20	91.94	92.80	94.78	95.21	95.41	95.23	95.49	95.44	95.59	95.92	96.05
1986	96.25	96.60	96.73	97.67	97.85	97.79	97.52	97.82	98.30	98.45	99.29	99.62
1987	100.0	100.4	100.6	101.8	101.9	101.9	101.8	102.1	102.4	102.9	103.4	103.3
1988	103.3	103.7	104.1	105.8	106.2	106.6	106.7	107.9	108.4	109.5	110.0	110.3
1989	111.0	111.8	112.3	114.3	115.0	115.4	115.5	115.8	116.6	117.5	118.5	118.8
1990	119.5	120.2	121.4	125.1	126.2	126.7	126.8	128.1	129.3	130.3	130.0	129.9
1991	130.2	130.9	131.4	133.1	133.5	134.1	133.8	134.1	134.6	135.1	135.6	135.7
1992	135.6	136.3	136.7	138.8	139.3	139.3	138.8	138.9	139.4	139.9	139.7	139.2
1993	137.9	138.8	139.3	140.6	141.1	141.0	140.7	141.3	141.9	141.8	141.6	141.9
1994	141.3	142.1	142.5	144.2	144.7	144.7	144.0	144.7	145.0	145.2	145.3	146.0
1995	146.0	146.9	147.5	149.0	149.6	149.8	149.1	149.9	150.6	149.8	149.8	150.7
1996	150.2	150.9	151.5	152.6	152.9	153.0	152.4	153.1	153.8	153.8	153.9	154.4
1997	154.4	155.0	155.4	156.3	156.9	157.5	157.5	158.5	159.3	159.5	159.6	160.0
1998	159.5	160.3	160.8	162.6	–	–	–	–	–	–	–	–

Shares and unit trusts

If you give away identical shares, unit trusts, or other securities that you acquired all at the same time, the CGT rules apply in the same way as for any other asset. However, suppose you own shares in one company, all of the same type, but they were bought at different times; special rules are needed to identify which particular shares you are disposing of, so that you can use the correct initial value and indexation allowance (if applicable) in your calculations.

Gifts made on or after 6 April 1998

For gifts and other disposals you made before 6 April 1998, the problem of identifying which shares were being given away or sold was solved mainly by pooling all the identical shares and working out an average price and indexation allowance for the lot. With the introduction of the CGT taper, however, it is now important to know exactly when each asset was acquired. So, for gifts and other disposals made on or after 6 April 1998, the shares, unit trusts or other securities which you give away are matched to the ones you own in the following order:

- shares you bought on the same day
- shares purchased within the following 30 days. This rule was introduced to curb a practice called 'bed-and-breakfasting'. You used to be able to realise a capital gain or loss by selling shares one day and buying them back the next – such a move could be very tax-efficient (see page 148). Now, you will need to leave at least 30 days between selling the shares and buying them back – a risky strategy when the stockmarket might move against you. However, there are alternative ways to bed–and–breakfast (see page 148)
- shares bought on or after 6 April 1998, identifying with the most recent acquisitions first – this is called a last–in–first–out (LIFO) basis
- shares in your '1982 pool' (see Batch 3, page 86)
- shares in your '1965 pool' (see Batch 4, page 86)
- shares you acquired before 6 April 1965, starting with the shares you bought most recently – i.e. LIFO basis. You can opt to have quoted shares treated as part of your 1965 pool instead.

There are two important points to note about the rules for identifying shares (and unit trusts and other securities):

- you must keep accurate records of your share purchases and sales, recording the dates of transactions, quantity and price of the shares involved
- the LIFO rules tend to minimise the amount of taper relief which you can claim.

EXAMPLE 7.7

Connie received 300 Halifax shares when the building society was demutualised in June 1997 and she bought further Halifax shares as follows:

9 April 1998	1,700 shares
2 November 1998	500 shares
16 July 1999	700 shares

In October 1999, she decides to give half her Halifax shares to her niece, Harriet. The 1,600 shares she gives away are matched in the following order:

16 July 1999	700 shares
2 November 1998	500 shares
9 April 1998	400 shares
Total	1,600 shares

Any subsequent gifts or other disposals would be matched against the remaining 1,300 shares bought on 9 April 1998 and then her original 300 shares.

Gifts made before 6 April 1998

For gifts or other disposals you made before 6 April 1998, the old identification rules apply. Your shareholding was divided into a maximum of five 'batches':

- *Batch 1* Your disposal is matched first to shares which you bought on the same day as the disposal. You cannot claim any indexation allowance.

- *Batch 2*   Next, your disposal is matched to shares which you bought within ten days before the disposal. You cannot claim any indexation allowance.
- *Batch 3*   Next, the disposal is matched to a 'pool' made up of all shares you acquired on or after 6 April 1982. To find the initial value of the shares and your indexation allowance, you need to work out the value of the shares after indexation *for the pool as a whole* (see Example 7.8 below).
- *Batch 4*   Next, the disposal is matched to a 'pool' made up of all the shares you bought in the period 6 April 1965 up to 5 April 1982. Again, to value the shares, you need to look at the pool as a whole. The indexation allowance is calculated only from March 1982, but based either on the actual purchases you made or on the value at 31 March 1982, unless you have elected to have all your assets rebased to this date (see page 78).
- *Batch 5*   Finally, the disposal is matched to any shares which you acquired before 6 April 1965, starting with the shares you bought most recently and working backwards. You can opt to have quoted shares treated as part of batch 4 instead.

EXAMPLE 7.8

In January 1997, Gerald gave his sister Dot 1,000 shares in a company, valued at £3,000. These are part of a holding which Gerald originally acquired in two lots: 1,000 shares for £1,500 in June 1982 and 2,000 shares for £4,000 in March 1988. The shares form a 'batch 3 pool'. The initial value of the pool after indexation is worked out as follows:

Cost of 1,000 shares bought in June 1982	£1,500
plus indexation allowance for period June 1982 to	
January 1997 (0.886 x £1,500)	£1,329
plus cost of 2,000 shares bought in March 1988	£4,000
plus indexation allowance for period March 1988 to	
January 1997 (0.483 x £4,000)	£1,932
Indexed value of pool	£8,761

Gerald gave away 1,000 of the 3,000 shares in the pool. The indexed value of the shares he gave away is deemed to be 1000/3000 x £8,761 = £2,920. (The indexed value of the shares remaining in the pool is 2000/3000 x £8,761 = £5,841 as at January 1997 – further indexation allowance will accrue up to the time Gerald disposes of these shares or April 1998 if this is sooner – after that the pool will be 'closed'.) Gerald's chargeable gain on the gift to Dot is worked out as follows:

Value of shares at the time of the gift	£3,000
less indexed value of the shares	£2,920
Chargeable gain	£80

How much tax?

If you are deemed to have made a chargeable gain on an asset you give away, there could be some tax to pay, but not necessarily. Everyone has a tax-free slice – more formally called the 'annual exempt amount'. This means that the first slice of chargeable gains which you make each year is tax-free. In 1999–2000, you can have net chargeable gains of £7,100 before any CGT becomes payable. The tax-free slice for earlier years is shown in Table 7.4.

Table 7.4   Tax-free slice for capital gains

Tax year	Tax-free slice
1988–9	£5,000
1989–90	£5,000
1990–1	£5,000
1991–2	£5,500
1992–3	£5,800
1993–4	£5,800
1994–5	£5,800
1995–6	£6,000
1996–7	£6,300
1997–8	£6,500
1998–9	£6,800
1999-2000	£7,100

Claiming allowable losses

If you make a loss on something you give away or otherwise dispose of, you can set the loss against gains you have made on other assets in the same tax year. Alternatively, you can carry the loss forward to set against gains made in a future year.

Since 6 April 1998, where you make a gift you deduct any losses you are claiming before applying the CGT taper and before deducting the tax-free slice. There are two drawbacks to this approach:

- losses, as well as gains, are reduced by the taper relief. But you do set off the losses in the way which benefits you most. This means, if you have made gains on several assets in the same year, setting losses against the gain(s) which qualify for the lowest taper relief – see Example 7.9
- where you are carrying forward losses made in an earlier year, you can continue to carry forward the losses if your net gains for the year come to no more than the tax-free slice. This prevents the tax-free slice being wasted. But, if your gains for the year come to more than the tax-free slice, you must set the carried-forward losses against the gains until they are reduced to the amount of the tax-free slice. Because this happens before applying taper relief, part of the loss relief is effectively wasted – see Example 7.10.

Where you made the disposal before 6 April 1998, losses made in the same tax year were claimed after deducting indexation allowance but before the tax-free slice; losses carried forward from an earlier year were deducted after subtracting the tax-free slice for the year. But there was no need to claim any more in losses than was needed to reduce the gains to the amount of the tax-free slice. This ensured that no allowances or reliefs were wasted.

EXAMPLE 7.9

In November 2003, Liam gives two plots of land to his son. The first was inherited in 1989. The gain on this plot after indexation allowance but before taper relief is £20,300. He qualifies for six years' taper relief on this gain. This means the gain can be reduced by 20 per cent.

Liam bought the second plot in September 1999. The gain on this is £4,500 before taper relief. He has held the land for three complete tax years, which qualifies him for 5 per cent taper relief.

Liam is carrying forward losses of £3,000 which he made on share sales several years ago. Consider the impact of setting these losses against each gain:

Losses set against gain on plot 1

Gain on plot 1	£20,300
Less loss relief	£3,000
Gain on plot 1 before taper relief	£17,300
Less taper relief for plot 1 @ 20%	£3,460
Plus gain on plot 2	£4,500
Less taper relief for plot 2 @ 5%	£225
Chargeable gains after loss relief and taper relief	£18,115

Losses set against gain on plot 2

Gain on plot 2	4,500
Less loss relief	£3,000
Gain on plot 2 before taper relief	£1,500
Less taper relief for plot 2 @ 5%	£75
Plus gain on plot 1	£20,300
Less taper relief for plot 1 @ 20%	£4,060
Chargeable gains after loss relief and taper relief	£17,665

Liam has lower chargeable gains and so pays less tax if he sets his carried-forward losses against the gain on plot 2 – in other words, the gain which qualifies for the lowest rate of taper relief. This is because taper relief reduces the losses by less.

EXAMPLE 7.10

In 2003-4, Sally has gains before taper relief of £8,500 and carried-forward losses of £1,300. We shall assume that the tax-free slice for the year is £7,900.

Sally must set enough of her carried-forward losses against the gains to reduce them to the level of the tax-free slice. In other words: £8,500 – £600 = £7,900. She qualifies for 10 per cent taper relief on her gains, reducing them to 90% x £7,900 = £7,110. But this is now £790 less than her tax-free slice for the year, so £790 of her reliefs have been wasted. She pays no tax on her gains and continues to carry forward the remaining £700 of losses.

If instead Sally had made gains of only £7,900 for the tax year, there would have been no tax to pay on them because they would be covered by the tax-free slice, but she would have continued to carry forward the full £1,300 of losses.

Working out the tax bill

If, after following these steps, you are left with a gain, there will be tax to pay. CGT is charged at two rates corresponding to the savings rate and higher rate of income tax, which are 20 per cent and 40 per cent, respectively, in 1999–2000. (Before April 1999, capital gains tax was levied at three rates corresponding to the lower, basic and higher rates of income tax.) To see which rate applies to you, add your taxable gains (after all the adjustments described above) to your taxable *income* for the year. The result of this sum tells you what rate of CGT is payable:

Table 7.5   Tax rate on chargeable gains 1999–2000

This tax rate applies	If your gains plus taxable income equal:
20 per cent	Up to £28,000
40 per cent	More than £28,000

If your taxable income is below the threshold given in Table 7.5 and adding the gain to the income takes the total above the threshold, you will pay the 20 per cent tax rate on part of your gain and the 40 per cent rate on the rest. For example, if you have taxable income of

£27,500 in the 1999–2000 tax year and taxable gains of £1,000 (making a total of £28,500), you would pay 20 per cent CGT on £500 of the gain and 40 per cent CGT on the £500 of gain which lies above the higher-rate threshold.

EXAMPLE 7.11

Frederick made a chargeable gain of £5,766 on the unit trusts he gives to Colin (see page 71). But after taking account of chargeable gains on other assets he has disposed of during the tax year, Frederick still has £6,000 of his tax-free slice unused. He can set this against the gift to Colin, which means there will be no CGT to pay.

EXAMPLE 7.12

In the 1999–2000 tax year, Emily has net chargeable gains of £7,929. She deducts the tax-free slice of £7,100, leaving taxable gains of £829. Emily's taxable income for the year is £27,600. The tax on her gains is worked out as follows:

Slice of gains in excess of £28,000 threshold	£429
Slice of gain within basic-rate band	£400
CGT at 40 per cent on £429	£171.60
CGT at 20 per cent on £400	£80.00
Total CGT bill	£251.60

Hold-over relief

With a few gifts you make, you could face bills for both CGT and IHT at the time the gift is made. Alternatively, you might face a CGT bill and have to use some or all of an IHT exemption which could trigger an IHT bill on a later gift. 'Hold-over relief' lets you avoid this potential for a double tax bill. The way it works is that, instead of being treated as having realised a gain on the asset you give away, you – in effect – give away your CGT liability along with the asset. Gifts which qualify for this relief must be made between individuals or trusts, and include:

- gifts which count as chargeable gifts for inheritance tax purposes (see Chapter 8) or would do so if they were not covered by the yearly tax-free exemption (see page 66). Gifts which are potentially exempt transfers (PETs) (see page 68) do not qualify for relief, unless they become chargeable because the person making the gift dies within seven years
- gifts for the public benefit of land, buildings, a work of art and so on (see page 64)
- gifts to political parties (see page 64)
- gifts made from accumulation-and-maintenance trusts at the time a beneficiary becomes entitled to the trust property or a life interest in it (see Chapter 10).

Hold-over relief is not given automatically. If you are making a gift to a person, both you and that person jointly claim the relief. If you are putting the gift into trust, only you need claim. Relief is given in the following way. The chargeable gain you have made on the asset up to the time of the gift is worked out. That amount is deducted from your total chargeable gains for the year – so you pay no CGT on the gain. The chargeable gain on the asset is also deducted from the recipient's initial value of the gift. This increases the likelihood of a chargeable gain when the recipient comes to dispose of the gift (though whether or not any tax would be payable then would depend on the availability of reliefs and exemptions, such as unused tax-free slice or further hold-over relief). For the purposes of calculating CGT taper relief when the recipient eventually disposes of the asset, the clock starts ticking from the date on which the recipient became the new owner of the asset.

Before 14 March 1989, hold-over relief applied to a much wider range of gifts, including those which counted as PETs under the IHT legislation. The restrictions now applying to the relief mean that it is mainly useful when you are making gifts to a discretionary trust (see page 139).

Hold-over relief may be clawed back if the person receiving the gift ceases to be a UK resident within five years of the gift being made. In that case, the person who made the gift could get an unexpected demand for CGT. If there is a possibility that the person to whom you are making the gift might move abroad, you could take out insurance to cover the possible CGT bill.

Giving away the family business

Hold-over relief is also available when you give away assets used in your business or shares in a family company. Relief must be claimed jointly by both the giver and the recipient. It works by enabling the giver to deduct the gain which would otherwise be payable from their chargeable gains, and the recipient deducts the same amount from the initial value at which he or she receives the assets or shares.

If the assets concerned have not been used in the business for the whole time that they were owned by the giver, then the amount of hold-over relief available may be scaled down proportionately (and the relevant period of ownership includes any time before 31 March 1982).

If hold-over relief is available on the assets anyway because they are subject to an IHT charge (see above) then the IHT-related hold-over relief applies rather than the business-related relief. Similarly, if the assets or shares qualify for 'retirement relief' (which until the year 2003 reduces or eliminates a CGT bill that would otherwise be payable when you dispose of your business in order to retire[22]), this will be given in preference to hold-over relief.

Hold-over relief can also be claimed on gifts of agricultural property. If the land or property is not currently in use as part of your business, then relief may still be granted if the property also qualifies for relief from IHT (see page 110).

If you give away or otherwise dispose of business assets, a higher than normal rate of taper relief applies in respect of periods since April 1998 during which you held the asset (see Table 7.6).

---

[22]Retirement relief is outside the scope of this book. For further details see, for example, *Which? Way to Save Tax*. Which? Books, published annually in autumn.

Table 7.6 CGT taper relief for business assets

If you have held the asset for this many complete tax years after 5 April 1998:	Your net chargeable gain is reduced by:	Only this percentage of your gain counts as chargeable:	For example, a net chargeable gain of £5,000 is reduced to:
0	No reduction	100%	£5,000
1	7.5%	92.5%	£4,625
2	15%	85%	£4,250
3	22.5%	77.5%	£3,875
4	30%	70%	£3,500
5	37.5%	62.5%	£3,125
6	45%	55%	£2,750
7	52.5%	47.5%	£2,375
8	60%	40%	£2,000
9	67.5%	32.5%	£1,625
10 or more	75%	25%	£1,250

For the purpose of taper relief, business assets are broadly defined as:

- something used by an individual, partnership or qualifying company (basically, a trading company of which you hold at least 25 per cent of the voting rights or you hold at least 5 per cent of the voting rights and you are a full-time employee or director) for the purpose of trade
- something you were required to have as a result of your employment
- shares in a qualifying company.

Where something is used partly for business and partly privately, the gain will be divided pro rata and the appropriate taper relief applied to each part.

If you are planning to give away your business or farm, you should seek advice from your accountant and solicitor.

Telling the taxman

If you receive a tax return asking about income and gains you have made in 1998–9, give the information asked for and send the return to your tax office by 30 September 1999 if you want your tax office to work out the tax for you, or by 31 January 2000 if you are happy to work out your own tax bill. For gains made in 1999–2000, you have until 31 January 2001 to submit details to your tax office.

If you don't receive a tax return, since 6 April 1995 you have just six months from the end of the tax year in which you made any chargeable gains to tell your tax office. For example, if you owe tax on gains made in 1998-9, you must notify your tax office by 5 October 1999. It will then send you a tax return to complete. Under self-assessment, where tax returns are sent out after 31 October, you have a full three months to send them back, rather than being tied to the normal 31 January deadline. If you have not made any chargeable gains, there is no requirement for you to report any disposals to your tax office.

If you don't let the Revenue know about chargeable gains you have made, you can be fined up to the amount of the tax due and unpaid by 31 January following the end of the tax year in which the gains were made. (If you pay the tax on time, you can't be fined, even if you still haven't given the tax office details of the gains.)

You are required to keep a record of any information needed to calculate your tax bill. The information may be original documents or copies and, by law, must be kept for one year following the date on which you filed your tax return with your tax office. Your tax office can ask to see these documents. However, it is prudent to hold on to your records for longer than this, because, if you discover an error, you can go back up to five years from 31 January following the year of assessment to claim back tax overpaid.

EXAMPLE 7.13

Unexpectedly, Emily did not receive a tax return for the 1998–9 tax year. However, she knows that she has some capital gains tax to pay. She must tell her tax office by 5 October 1999, so that it can send her a tax return to complete. Emily or her accountant should calculate the amount of CGT due and ensure that it is paid by 31 January 2000. Alternatively, Emily can ask her tax office to work out the tax bill but if the return reaches the office after 30 September 1999 it cannot guarantee to let Emily know the amount of CGT due in time for the 31 January 2000 payment date. To avoid any fine, Emily should pay an estimated amount by 31 January 2000 even if she does not know the exact bill by then.

Chapter 8

Inheritance tax on lifetime gifts

A TAX NO ONE PAYS?

'Do you have to pay any inheritance tax when you give me Hadley Hall?' asked Albert.

'It's none of your business,' snapped Daisy, 'though if you'd bothered to learn anything useful you'd know that there's no inheritance tax on a gift from one person to another – it's a PET! I suppose you think that's a furry animal.'

'As it happens I *do* know about PETs,' retorted Albert, 'and there could be a tax bill – what's more I could end up having to pay it. So it really is my business too.'

Prior to both the 1999 and 1998 Budgets, rumours abounded that the government would make radical changes to the inheritance tax (IHT) system, closing off exemptions and killing the much-loved PET. The Budgets, when they came, were pure anti-climax and the inheritance tax regime, bar a little tinkering, has – so far – been left entirely intact.

Chapter 6 listed the many exemptions from IHT for gifts made during your lifetime – so many in fact that IHT is sometimes referred to as a voluntary tax. That is not quite true. Two types of gift could result in an IHT bill during the giver's lifetime:

- gifts to or from a company
- gifts to a 'discretionary trust' (see Chapter 10).

Gifts from one person to another, which counted as potentially exempt transfers (PETs) (see page 68) when they were made, can also cause an IHT bill if the person making the gift dies within seven years. You must also be careful if you make 'gifts with reservation': that is, giving away something from which you continue to benefit.

Gifts which are taxable when they are made

The scope of inheritance tax

The forerunner of IHT was called capital transfer tax (CTT). The two taxes were virtually the same, with one very important difference: CTT applied to virtually *all* gifts, whereas under the IHT system, gifts between *individuals* (and certain types of trust) count as PETs, which are tax-free as long as the giver survives for seven years after making the gift. However, even under the present system, some gifts – that is, those which are *not* between individuals (and certain trusts) – can prompt an immediate tax bill. In tax language, such gifts are called 'chargeable transfers' and they comprise mainly gifts involving companies and gifts to discretionary trusts. In this book, chargeable transfers are also referred to as 'chargeable gifts'.

How a chargeable transfer is taxed

IHT does not apply to each gift you make in isolation. It is based on all the chargeable transfers you have made over the last seven years. Adding all these gifts together gives you a 'cumulative total' – called your 'running total' in this book. The first slice of the running total – up to £231,000 for the 1999–2000 tax year – is tax-free. You pay tax only on gifts which take you above that limit. The tax-free slice is normally increased each tax year in line with inflation up to the previous September, but the changes have sometimes been more erratic: in 1992–3, the tax-free slice was increased by more than inflation; in the two subsequent years it was not increased at all; in 1996–7, there was a further very large increase, followed by another increase which exceeded inflation in 1997–8 (see Table 8.1).

The IHT rate on lifetime gifts is set with reference to the rate of tax which may apply to your estate when you die (see Chapter 13). The death rate for the 1998–9 tax year is 40 per cent; the lifetime rate is 20 per cent.

Table 8.1 Rates of inheritance tax

Tax year	Tax-free slice	Rate of tax on running total in excess of the tax-free slice	
		Death rate	Lifetime rate
1988–9	£110,000	40%	20%
1989–90	£118,000	40%	20%
1990–91	£128,000	40%	20%
1991–2	£140,000	40%	20%
1992–3	£150,000	40%	20%
1993–4	£150,000	40%	20%
1994–5	£150,000	40%	20%
1995–6	£154,000	40%	20%
1996–7	£200,000	40%	20%
1997–8	£215,000	40%	20%
1998–9	£223,000	40%	20%
1999–2000	£231,000	40%	20%

Tax due on a lifetime gift can be paid either by the person (or trust or company) making the gift or by the person (or trust or company) receiving the gift. If the person making the gift pays, the tax itself counts as part of the gift, which increases the value of the transfer to be taxed. A gift where the giver pays the tax is called a 'net gift'; if the recipient pays the tax, it is called a 'gross gift'. You can work out how much tax is due on a net or gross gift using the calculators below and overleaf.

CALCULATOR FOR INHERITANCE TAX ON A NET GIFT, 1999–2000

A What is your running total before making the gift (including any tax paid by you)?

B Work out the tax due on your running total:
If **A** is £231,000 or less, the tax due is 0.
If **A** is more than £231,000, the tax due is 20% x [**A** – £231,000].

C Subtract **B** from **A**. This gives you your net running total.

D Enter value of gift – use the amount the recipient will receive.

E Add **C** and **D**. This gives you your new net running total.

F Work out the tax due on your new running total:
If **E** is £231,000 or less, the tax is 0.
If **E** is more than £231,000, the tax due is 25% x [**E** – £231,000].

G Subtract **B** from **F**. This is the amount of tax (to be paid by the giver) on the current gift.

CALCULATOR FOR INHERITANCE TAX ON A GROSS GIFT, 1999–2000

A What is your running total before making the gift (including any tax paid by you)?

B Work out the tax due on your running total:
If **A** is £231,000 or less, the tax due is 0.
If **A** is more than £231,000, the tax due is 20% x [**A** – £231,000].

C Enter the current gift – use the amount you are giving.

D Find your new running total by adding **C** and **A**.

E Work out the tax due on your new running total:
If **D** is £231,000 or less, the tax due is 0.
If **D** is more than £231,000, the tax due is 20% x [**D** – £231,000].

F Subtract **B** from **E**. This is the amount of tax (to be paid by the recipient) on the current gift.

EXAMPLE 8.1

Frederick has a grown-up daughter, Louise, who suffers from a slight mental disability. She lives largely independently and has a modest income from a job in a supermarket, but she would not be able to cope with large sums of money or complicated planning for the future.

Frederick wants to make sure that Louise will always be financially secure and to provide a 'last resort' emergency fund which would be available to his son Colin if the need arose. Frederick decides to set up a discretionary trust for the benefit of his children, making himself and his sister the trustees who will decide when Louise or Colin need help and how much help they should receive. (For more about discretionary trusts, see Chapter 10.)

Frederick sets up the trust in October 1999 with a gift of £70,000. He will pay any tax due on this, so it is a net gift. As Frederick has not used any of his annual exemption of £3,000 for 1999–2000 (see page 66), only £67,000 counts as a chargeable transfer. Over the seven years from November 1990 to October 1999, he has made other chargeable transfers of £173,000. He uses the calculator for net gifts (see page 99) to work out his inheritance tax position as follows:

A Frederick's running total before making the gift (including any tax paid by him).	£173,000
B Tax due on his running total: If **A** is £231,000 or less, the tax due is 0 If **A** is more than £231,000, the tax due is 20% x [**A** – £231,000]	£0
C Subtract **B** from **A**. This gives you Frederick's net running total	£173,000
D Enter value of gift – the amount the trust will receive	£67,000
E Add **C** and **D**. This gives Frederick's new net running total	£240,000
F Tax due on his new running total: If **E** is £231,000 or less, the tax is 0 If **E** is more than £231,000, the tax due is 25% x [**E** – £231,000] (i.e. $\frac{1}{4}$ x £9,000)	£2,250
G Subtract **B** from **F**. This is the amount of tax (to be paid by Frederick) on the gift to the trust.	£2,250

Frederick's gift to the trust is made up of the £70,000 plus £2,250 he pays in tax – £72,250 in total.

EXAMPLE 8.2

Suppose, in Example 8.1 above, that Frederick decided to pay £70,000 into the trust, but to leave the trust to pay any tax. In this case, the chargeable transfer of £67,000 would be a *gross* gift. Using the calculator for gross gifts (see page 100), the inheritance tax position would be:

A Frederick's running total before making the gift (including any tax paid by him)	£173,000
B Tax due on his running total: If **A** is £231,000 or less, the tax due is 0. If **A** is more than £231,000, the tax due is 20% x [**A** – £231,000]	£0
C Enter the current gift – the amount Frederick is giving	£67,000
D Frederick's new running total is found by adding **C** and **A**	£240,000
E Tax due on his new running total: If **D** is £231,000 or less, the tax due is 0. If **D** is more than £231,000, the tax due is 20% x [**D** – £231,000]. (i.e. 20% x £9000)	£1,800
F Subtract **B** from **E**. This is the amount of tax (to be paid by the trust) on the gift to the trust.	£1,800

The trust would receive £70,000, but £1,800 would have to be used to pay the IHT bill due on the transfer.

Death within seven years

Tax on a lifetime gift which is a chargeable transfer is usually charged at a rate of 20 per cent (in 1999–2000). But, if the person making the gift dies within three years, the gift is reassessed and tax is charged at the full death rate current at the time of death (i.e. 40 per cent for 1999–2000). If the giver dies more than three years but less than seven years after making the gift, the gift is still reassessed for tax but at less than the full death rate. Table 8.2 shows the rates which would apply.

The extra tax due will be charged to the person who received the gift, but if they cannot or will not pay, the giver's estate must pay the bill.

Table 8.2   New tax rate if giver dies within seven years of making a gift

Years between gift and death	% of full death rate which applies	% rate of tax on the gift (at 1998–9 rates)
Up to 3	100	40
More than 3 and up to 4	80	32
More than 4 and up to 5	60	24
More than 5 and up to 6	40	16
More than 6 up to 7	20	8
More than 7	0	no extra tax

At first sight, you might assume that there will never be any extra tax to pay if the giver dies more than five years after making the chargeable transfer, since the rate of tax which would then apply (16 per cent assuming 1999–2000 rates) is lower than the 20 per cent rate at which tax is paid on lifetime gifts. However, the position is not so simple: in reassessing the gift, it is looked at in relation to the running total at the time the gift was made; since PETs may also be reassessed (see page 104) when the giver dies, a PET made within the seven-year period but before the chargeable transfer being considered would increase the running total. Also, bear in mind that the original tax on the gift was charged at the rates applicable at the time of the gift, whereas tax due on reassessment is charged at the rates applicable at the time of death – and a change in rates may result in extra tax becoming due. Equally a relaxation in IHT rates may seem to imply a reduction in the tax bill – see Example 8.3 on page 106. But none of the tax paid at the time the gift was made is refundable. For a summary of tax-free slices and tax rates applicable in earlier years, see Table 8.1 on page 99.

Potentially exempt transfers (PETs)

Most of the gifts that you make during your lifetime are free of IHT, even if they are not covered by one of the specific exemptions outlined in Chapter 6, because they will count as potentially exempt transfers (PETs). As the name suggests, these gifts are exempt but with a proviso: the giver must survive for seven years after making the gift. The purpose of this rule is to prevent people escaping tax on their estates by giving away their possessions shortly before death.

If the giver does die within seven years of making a gift, the gift loses its exempt status and is reassessed as a chargeable gift. This has two effects, which are quite separate though unfortunately often confused:

- first, because the PET is now treated as chargeable, the taxman steps back in time and asks: at the time this gift was made, given that we now know it is chargeable, should any tax have been paid? What happens if the answer is 'yes' is described under 'How the PET is taxed' below
- second, because the PET has become a chargeable gift, it enters into your running total, which may mean that extra tax becomes due on subsequent chargeable gifts, other PETs being reassessed and the estate left at the time of death – see Example 8.3 on page 106.

How the PET is taxed

If the giver dies within seven years, the PET is treated as if it had originally been a chargeable transfer. Of course, this does not necessarily mean tax is due, because:

- in the tax year you made the gift, you might not have used your yearly £3,000 tax-free exemption (see page 66). And, if you had not used the exemption in the previous year either, you might have the scope to give up to £6,000 in that tax year in chargeable gifts without having any tax to pay

- as with any other gift which might be taxable, it is not looked at in isolation. It is included in your running total over the seven years up to the date of the gift in question. Only if the running total exceeds the relevant tax-free slice will any tax become due. In the case of a reassessed PET, the relevant tax-free slice is the amount in force at the time of death (not at the time the gift was made) – i.e. £231,000 if the giver died in the 1999–2000 tax year.

It is important to note that PETs up to seven years before death are reassessed and gifts in the seven years up to the making of the PET are looked at in deciding whether tax is due. This means that gifts made during the *14* years before death are relevant.

If the running total up to the making of the reassessed PET does come to more than the tax-free slice at the time of death, then IHT is due at the rates current at the time of death – i.e. 40 per cent in 1999-2000. However, if the giver died more than three years after making the gift, the amount of tax payable is reduced by the effect of what is called 'taper relief'. Table 8.3 shows the effect of this relief.

Table 8.3   How IHT taper relief reduces tax on a reassessed PET

Years between making the PET and death	% of full death rate which applies	Effective % rate of tax on the gift (at 1998–9 rates)
Up to 3	100	40
More than 3 and up to 4	80	32
More than 4 and up to 5	60	24
More than 5 and up to 6	40	16
More than 6 and up to 7	20	8
More than 7	0	no tax

Bear in mind that taper relief only reduces any tax due on the reassessed PET. If there is no tax payable on the PET (for example, because the running total including the PET is less than the tax-free slice), then taper relief has no relevance. And taper relief cannot be used to reduce tax on the estate of the deceased giver, even if that tax bill was created or increased because of the inclusion of the reassessed PET in the running total up to the time of death.

Who pays the tax?

Any tax which becomes due on a reassessed PET is first charged to the person who received the gift. If he or she cannot or will not pay, the late giver's estate must pay the bill. It is possible to take out insurance to cover the potential tax bill on a PET.

EXAMPLE 8.3

Godfrey dies on 1 January 2000 leaving an estate of £150,000. He made the following gifts during his lifetime (assuming the annual tax-free exemptions have already been used in each case):

1 January 1990	Chargeable transfer	£60,000 paid into a discretionary trust
1 January 1992	Chargeable transfer	£50,000 paid into a discretionary trust
1 February 1993	Chargeable transfer	£58,000 paid into a discretionary trust
1 June 1995	PET	£100,000 given to nephew, John

On his death, chargeable transfers and PETs made within the seven years before death – i.e. in the period 2 January 1993 to 1 January 2000 – are reassessed as follows:

- chargeable transfer made on 1 February 1993. Tax was originally paid in 1992–3 on a running total of £60,000 + £50,000 + £58,000 = £168,000. The tax-free slice then was £150,000 and the trust paid tax at 20 per cent on the £18,000 of the February 1993 gift which exceeded that slice – i.e. tax of 20 per cent x £18,000 = £3,600. When the gift is reassessed on Godfrey's death, there is no tax to be paid because the running total of £168,000 is less than the tax-free slice in force at the time of death – i.e. £231,000. However, no refund is allowed of the tax already paid in Godfrey's lifetime
- PET made on 1 June 1995. No tax was charged on the PET at the time it was made. When it is reviewed on Godfrey's death, the PET becomes the top slice of £100,000 on a running total of £60,000 + £50,000 + £58,000 + £100,000 = £268,000. Earlier gifts have used up £168,000 of the tax-free slice of £231,000. £63,000 of the PET exhausts the remaining tax-free slice. This leaves £37,000 to be taxed

at the death rate of 40 per cent. So tax is initially calculated as 40% x £37,000 = £14,800. However, taper relief applies because the PET was more than three years before Godfrey's death. Only 60 per cent of the tax is payable – i.e. 60% x £14,800 = £8,880.

Although more properly the subject of Chapter 13, it is worth noting here what impact the reassessed chargeable transfers and PETs have on tax on the estate. The estate counts as the top slice of £150,000 on a running total of £58,000 + £100,000 + £150,000 = £308,000. The earlier gifts use up £158,000 of the £231,000 tax-free slice. £73,000 of the estate uses up the remaining part of the tax-free slice. This leaves £77,000 of the estate to be taxed at 40 per cent – i.e. 40% x £77,000 = £30,800. Note that taper relief is not relevant to this tax bill which is payable in full – by the estate, unless the will specifies otherwise.

Fall in value

There is some tax relief if the value of a PET or chargeable transfer has fallen since the time it was first made. Whoever is paying the tax is allowed to deduct the fall in value from the original value of the gift. Bear in mind, however, that the original value of a gift was the loss to the giver *not* the value to the recipient, so even a large percentage fall in the value of the item in the recipient's hands may have only a small impact on the value of the item for IHT purposes (see Example 8.4). The fall-in-value relief is not given automatically; the person paying the tax must make a claim to the Capital Taxes Office.*

EXAMPLE 8.4

In September 1997, Dorothy gave her niece, Charlotte, one of a pair of rare antique vases. As a pair, the vases had a market price of £110,000, but individually they were each worth only £40,000. The value of the gift was the loss to Dorothy, in other words, the difference between the market price of the pair and the price of the remaining vase: £110,00 – £40,000 = £70,000. The gift counted as a potentially exempt transfer (PET) and so there was no tax to pay.

In February 2000, Dorothy dies and Charlotte receives a demand for tax on the gift of the vase. She has the vase valued by a local dealer who puts a market price of only £35,000 on the vase now. Charlotte agrees to the reduced value of the gift which is worked out as the original loss to the giver less the fall in value: £70,000 – £5,000 = £65,000.

Tax now due on the gift is calculated as follows. Just before she made the gift to Charlotte, in September 1997, Dorothy's cumulative total of gifts, including other PETs that have become chargeable since her death, came to £180,000. Adding the value of the vase brings the total to £180,000 + £65,000 = £245,000. This is £14,000 more than the 1999–2000 tax-free slice of £231,000, so IHT is payable at 40% x £14,000 = £5,600. As fewer than three years have passed since Dorothy made the gift, taper relief does not apply.

Protection from IHT on a PET

Life insurance can be used to protect the person receiving a PET from a possible IHT bill (see page 197 for how this would work). The insurance could be taken out by the person making a PET, in which case the insurance would itself count as a gift but might qualify for one of the IHT exemptions (see Chapter 6). Another option would be for the person receiving the PET to pay premiums him or herself for a term insurance policy based on the life of the giver.

Life insurance can also be used in just the same way to protect the recipient of a gift that counts as a chargeable transfer from the possibility of an extra tax bill should the giver die within seven years.

For more information, seek advice from an insurance broker or an independent financial adviser.

Gifts with reservation

Problems can arise if you give something away but continue to benefit from it in some way. A 'gift with reservation' occurs in the following circumstances:

- if the person to whom you give the gift does not really take possession of it: for example, you might give a valuable painting to someone but insist that it carries on hanging in your home

- if you carry on deriving some benefit from the thing you give away unless you pay a full market rate – or the equivalent in kind – for your use of the asset. This might occur, for example, if you give your home to your children but you retain the right to live in part of the property rent-free. (See Chapter 15 for more about this.)

Special rules apply to gifts with reservation. However, if the gift is covered by one of the IHT exemptions outlined in Chapter 6 at the time the gift is made, the special rules do not normally apply and there is no IHT to pay. But you cannot claim the 'expenditure out of normal income' exemption against a gift with reservation and you cannot use your £3,000 yearly exemption against the gift at the time it is made.

Unless the gift counts as a chargeable transfer, there is no IHT to pay when the gift is made, but there may be later on. The special rules come into operation at the time the person who made the gift dies. If, at the time of death, the giver still benefited from the gift with reservation, the possessions they gave are treated as if they are still part of the giver's estate and were given away only at the time of death (see Chapter 13). If the giver stopped benefiting from the possessions some time before his or her death, the gift with reservation is treated as a PET made at the time the giver's benefit stopped. Provided that this was more than seven years before death, IHT will not apply. On the other hand, if that time was within the seven years before the giver's death, the normal PET rules apply and there may be an IHT bill on the gift. In the event that the giver had unused yearly exemption for the year in which the gift stopped being a gift with reservation, that can be set against the PET in the normal way.

If the gift with reservation counted as a chargeable transfer, IHT may have been paid when the gift was made – this would apply, say, to a gift you made to a discretionary trust. The special rules still apply when the giver dies, but other rules prevent IHT being payable twice over on the same gift. For example, suppose you give £10,000 to a discretionary trust designed to benefit your whole family, including yourself. Because you are a beneficiary of the trust, you are still able to benefit from the £10,000 so it counts as a gift with reservation. As a gift to a discretionary trust, it is a chargeable transfer on which IHT may be payable. But, if you continue to be a beneficiary of the trust right up to the time you die, the £10,000 will continue to be deemed as part of your estate and treated as if it was given outright to the trust only on the date of your death. At that time, the gift may again give rise to an IHT bill, but special rules give relief against the double charge (though not against other tax charges relating to the trust, see Chapter 10).

A gift is not a gift with reservation if you continue to benefit but you pay for the right to do so.

If you can carve up a possession which you intend to give so that you can keep a distinct part of it, you can give away the remainder without that part counting as a gift with reservation. However, your scope to adopt this approach to gifts of land has been severely limited by the Inland Revenue's reaction to the success of a tax case, Ingram and Another *v* Inland Revenue Commissioners. Lady Ingram owned the freehold to her house and land. She divided this into a rent-free lease which she kept and a separate freehold, subject to the lease, which she gave away (an arrangement known as a 'lease carve-out'). The Inland Revenue claimed that the gift of the freehold was a gift with reservation since Lady Ingram retained the right to live in the house without paying any rent. The case took nine years and finally reached the House of Lords. The Lords decided that the rent-free lease was *not* a reservation of benefit in relation to the gift of the freehold. This was a triumph for the taxpayer and looked set to open the way for many similar schemes. The Inland Revenue was not amused. In the 1999 Budget, new rules were introduced to ensure that such schemes are after all caught by the reservation of benefit rules. The new rules apply to gifts of an interest in land made on or after 9 March 1999.

Giving away the family business

If you pass on your business or farm during your lifetime, you may qualify for relief against IHT on the value of the transfer. Basic details of the schemes are given in Chapter 13, which look at passing on your business or farm in your will. The application of the scheme is broadly the same in the case of lifetime gifts, with one important exception outlined below.

Whether your gift of business or agricultural property counts as a PET or as a chargeable transfer, the relief will be clawed back, if:

- you die within seven years of making the gift, and
- the recipient no longer owns the business or farm, and
- the recipient does not fully re-invest the proceeds in – in the case of business property relief – a new business, or – in the case of agricultural property relief – a new farm.

Relief will also be clawed back if the recipient dies before you and no longer owns the business or farm.

In view of this clawback, it is extremely important that you plan carefully, and that you take expert advice from your accountant and a solicitor, before making a gift of part or all of your business or farm.

Telling the taxman

You do not have to tell the tax authorities about any gifts you make which count as PETs, but you should keep a record of all the gifts you make. Put a copy of the record where it would be found by whoever would handle your estate if you were to die – for example, in the same place as your will. It would be the responsibility of that person to pass these details on to the Capital Taxes Office so that PETs could be reassessed.

If you make gifts which count as chargeable transfers – i.e. gifts to discretionary trusts or involving companies – you do not need to tell the tax office, provided:

- your total chargeable transfers during the year come to no more than £10,000, and
- your running total of gifts during the last seven years comes to no more than £40,000.

If you have made a chargeable transfer that should be reported, you need to complete **form IHT100**, which is available from the Capital Taxes Office.

In the case of lifetime chargeable gifts, IHT is normally due to be paid six months after the end of the month in which the gift was made. But if the gift was made in the period 6 April to 1 October, tax is due on 30 April of the following year.

Should extra tax become payable on a chargeable gift, or should the PET become chargeable because of the death of the giver within seven years of making the gift, the tax is due six months after the end of the month in which the death occurs. In some limited cases, it may be possible to pay the tax in ten equal yearly instalments.

Chapter 9

Income tax and gifts

WHOSE TAX IS IT ANYWAY?

'I don't believe this,' Michael exploded, waving the tax assessment he had just opened. 'The Revenue have charged me income tax on Rebecca's savings account.'

Rebecca looked on quizzically. 'But you opened the account for me, Daddy. Isn't it mine any more?'

There is no income tax as such on a gift, but just as a gift to charity can affect the income tax position of the giver and the recipient, so too can gifts between individuals. If you are aware of the types of gift that affect income tax and the pitfalls to watch out for, you are then well placed to arrange your giving in the most tax-efficient way.

Gifts between husband and wife

Independent taxation

An important date in the tax calendar was 6 April 1990, because, from the 1990–1 tax year onwards, 'independent taxation' was introduced. A married couple had up to then been treated as a single unit for tax purposes, but now husband and wife are each treated as individuals responsible for their own tax. This means that:

- you are taxed on your own income, regardless of your spouse's income
- you claim your own tax allowances to set against your income

- you have your own tax-free slice for capital gains tax (CGT) purposes. (You also have your own inheritance tax – IHT – running total and exemptions, but this was the case even before independent taxation was introduced.)

Before independent taxation, it mattered little from an income tax point of view whether it was you or your husband or wife who owned the family assets – house, savings, and so on. It seems amazing in this age of equality that any income from such assets used always to be treated as that of the husband even if legally it belonged to the wife. Nowadays, the system is much fairer: your individual tax bills will take account of income from the assets that each of you in fact owns. This means that who owns what is important, and rearranging the family assets – for example, through gifts between husband and wife – could reduce the income tax bill of the family as a whole. Bear in mind that there is no CGT or IHT to pay on gifts between husband and wife, but the pattern in which you hold the family assets could affect IHT later on (see Chapter 14).

EXAMPLE 9.1

In August 1999, Ray inherits a substantial portfolio of corporate bonds and government stocks from his late aunt. The portfolio produces a healthy income which Ray welcomes, but he is dismayed at having to pay tax on it at his top rate of 40 per cent. His wife, Joyce, has no income or savings of her own, so it makes sense for Ray to give some of his investments to her. He transfers enough so that Joyce receives an investment income of around £4,335 — the amount of her unused personal allowance in 1999–2000. No IHT or CGT is payable on the gift from Ray to Joyce.

Although most of the investments pay out income with some tax already deducted, Joyce is able to claim the tax back, so the income is tax-free in her hands.

Jointly owned assets

Like many married couples, you may well have bank accounts, savings accounts and investments that are jointly held by you and your husband or wife. In England and Wales there are two ways of holding assets jointly: under a 'joint tenancy' or as 'tenants in common'. These are legal terms which can apply to any type of asset and not only to the way you share a home. (Different arrangements apply in Scotland – see page 116.)

Under a joint tenancy, you and your spouse both own the whole asset, you have identical interests in it, and you cannot sell or give away the asset without the agreement of the other person. In the event of one of you dying, the other automatically becomes the sole owner of the asset (though the deceased person's share still counts as part of his or her estate).

Under a tenancy in common, you and your spouse both have the right to enjoy or use the whole asset, but you each have your own distinct share in the asset and the shares need not be equal. On your death, your share of the asset does not automatically pass to your husband or wife and you can leave it to anyone you choose.

You can switch from owning an asset under a joint tenancy to a tenancy in common quite simply. The switch does not need to be recorded in any particular legal form – a simple written statement from one owner to the other would be sufficient. However, it is better for a joint statement to be agreed and signed by both owners. Switching from a tenancy in common to a joint tenancy requires a formal deed, which a solicitor can draw up for you.

For income tax purposes, the Inland Revenue will at first assume that any assets you hold jointly are held under a joint tenancy. This means that you will each be treated as receiving half of any income from the asset. If you want the income to be treated differently, you need to send your tax office a completed **form 17** setting out how the income is to be shared between you. You can get form 17 from your usual tax office or a local Tax Enquiry Centre.

However, be warned that the way the income is split for tax purposes *must* reflect the actual shares that you and your spouse have in the income-producing asset. You cannot just choose the most convenient income split if it does not match the real shares, and you cannot choose one split for income purposes and another for capital.

You should be prepared to provide the Inland Revenue with proof of the shares you each have in an asset and thus your share of the income. The proof might be copies of application forms or documents you signed when you first had the asset, or copies of deeds or letters stating the relative shares.

Consider giving some of your assets to your husband or wife, or giving away part of your share of an asset, if to do so would mean that together you pay less tax, as in the following circumstances:

- if one of you pays income tax and the other does not, give income-producing assets to the non-taxpayer (as in Example 9.1 on page 114.) But note that from April 1999 onwards, non-taxpayers can no longer reclaim the tax already deducted from income from shares, share-based unit trusts and similar investments. In 1999-2000, this type of income is paid with tax at 10 per cent already deducted. Higher-rate taxpayers have extra to pay, but for all other taxpayers there is neither more tax to pay nor any tax to reclaim

- if one of you pays tax at the higher rate and the other pays tax at the basic or lower rate, give income-producing assets (including shares, unit trusts and so on) to the taxpayer paying at the lowest rate. Income from most investments is paid with tax (at the savings rate of 20 per cent or at the shares rate of 10 per cent in 1999–2000) already deducted. Lower- and basic-rate taxpayers have no further tax to pay, but higher-rate taxpayers must pay extra tax

- if one of you regularly uses up your capital gains tax-free slice but the other does not, give assets whose value is expected to rise to the person with the unused slice.

Joint assets in Scotland

In Scotland, jointly owned assets are nearly always held as tenants in common – i.e. with each person owning a distinct share of the asset. However, if the owners have agreed on it, there can be a 'survivorship destination clause' written into the ownership documents. Like joint tenancy in England and Wales, the survivorship destination clause ensures that the share of a co-owner who dies automatically passes to the remaining owner(s) – even if the will stipulates that something different should happen. A survivorship destination can be cancelled only with the consent of all the owners and requires a formal deed which can be drawn up by a solicitor.

Gifts to children

A child is an individual for tax purposes and has his or her own personal tax allowance to set against any income. Many children do not make use of their allowance, so there is scope for reducing the family's overall tax bill by making gifts to a child. However, the tax rules are very strict in this area and any gift to a child needs to be carefully thought out if it is to have the desired income tax effect.

Gifts from parents

In general, if you give assets to your child and these produce income, the income will count as *yours* – not the child's. For example, if you invest some money in a building society for your son or daughter, interest earned will generally count as your interest. But the Inland Revenue makes a concession in the case of small amounts of income: up to £100 a year of income from assets given by a parent can count as income of the child. This concession applies to each parent, so the child could have up to £200 income from such gifts if both father and mother gave the maximum allowed.

Should you want to give more to your child without having to pay his or her tax bill, you have three choices, as follows:

- give assets which provide tax-free income
- give assets which produce capital gains rather than income
- put the assets into trust – see Chapter 10.

Tax-free income

If income from gifts you have made to your child comes to no more than £100 a year (£200 if you have spread the gifts equally between father and mother), and you want to make further gifts of investments, consider those which provide tax-free income: for example, certain National Savings investments and friendly society investments.

Two investments are especially designed for children: National Savings Children's Bonus Bonds and friendly society children's savings plans.

Children's Bonus Bonds

Children's Bonus Bonds can be bought by anyone over the age of 16 for anyone under 16. If children want to invest their own money in the bonds, they must enlist the help of their parents or some other adult. The bonds can be held until the child reaches age 21.

The minimum investment is £25, and each child can hold up to £1,000 of each previous issue of bonds, plus up to £1,000 of the current issue at the time this book went to press. The money invested earns a modest amount of interest, but a sizeable chunk of the return comes from bonuses which are added every five years. The interest for the next five years and the next bonus to be paid are fixed in advance and are guaranteed. On each five-year anniversary of a bond, the new interest and bonus rates are set. The return on the bonds is completely tax-free.

The bonds automatically mature when the holder reaches 21. They can also be cashed in earlier without penalty on any five-year anniversary. If a bond is cashed in at any other time, the holder must give one month's notice and will forgo the next bonus payment. No interest is paid on a bond which is cashed in during its first year.

The return on Children's Bonus Bonds is published regularly in newspapers, in magazines, such as *Which?,* or can be obtained from post offices which also stock application forms or the National Savings Internet site.★

Friendly society children's savings plans

Friendly society plans are basically ten-year life insurance policies. They offer little life cover and are intended mainly as savings vehicles. Since July 1991 friendly societies have been able to offer children's savings plans aimed at people under the age of 18 – these plans are often referred to as 'baby bonds'. Either the child can invest in the plan, or an adult can make investments on the child's behalf.

You pay regular premiums into the plan and the society invests these in a range of assets – shares, British government stocks, and so on. After ten years, you receive a lump sum, the size of which reflects the growth of the underlying investments (less various charges deducted by the society). Friendly society plans are very tax-efficient. The society pays no tax on the gains and income from the underlying investments. From 6 April 1999, when tax on dividends and distributions from shares and share-based unit trusts falls to 10 per cent and tax credits for most investors will no longer be available, friendly societies will still be able to reclaim the tax credit (also set at 10 per cent). They will be able to do this for five years up to 5 April 2004, ensuring that these savings plans are on an equal footing with other tax-efficient investments, such as Individual Savings Accounts. You pay no tax on the lump sum you receive when your friendly society plan matures.

The drawback is that you can invest only fairly small amounts in friendly society tax-free plans. The maximum investment is £270 a year (or £24.75 a month), and you can have only one such plan at a time. Charges can make large inroads into such small investments, so you should check the position before you invest.

Gains rather than income

Since the restrictions applying to gifts from a parent apply only to income, you can get round them by giving assets which are expected to produce a capital gain instead. Even a child is entitled to a yearly tax-free slice for capital gains tax purposes and, as Chapter 7 described, there are various other deductions which reduce or eliminate the tax liability.

Suitable gifts might be shares that pay low or no dividends, growth unit trusts, growth investment trusts (such as zero-dividend preference shares, commonly known as 'zeros'), collectors' items such as paintings and antiques, and so on.

EXAMPLE 9.2

Michael had not realised, when he opened a building society account for his daughter Rebecca, that income from the £20,000 he had placed in the account would count as his own for tax purposes.

He decides to close the account and put £1,000 into a National Savings Children's Bonus Bond for Rebecca and the rest into a growth unit trust for her.

A special type of trust

Another way in which you used to be able ensure that income from a gift you make to your child was not taxed as your income was to use a 'bare trust'. Trusts generally are described in Chapter 10, but a bare trust is very much simpler: the trustees (see page 124) simply hold the money or assets as nominees on behalf of the beneficiary (see page 125) and have no powers to do anything with the money or assets other than in accordance with the beneficiary's instructions.

In the case of a gift from parent to child, a bare trust works like this: you make the gift to your child, but you continue to hold it on his or her behalf. In the past, provided you did not pay any of the trust money or assets over to the child or use them for the benefit of your child, any income earned by the trust assets counted as the child's, not yours. However, concerned by increasing use of the bare trust arrangement, the government changed the rules in the 1999 Budget. For trusts set up on or after 9 March 1999, or for new funds added to existing bare trusts on or after that date, income earned counts as that of the parent, if the parent gave the assets held by the trust – though, as with other parental gifts, income up to just £100 does count as that of the child. Any capital gains count as the child's. In addition, where income has accumulated within a bare trust and has been taxed as that of the child, there will be tax to pay if the income is subsequently withdrawn from the trust.

Bare trusts are, therefore, less useful than in the past. And a major drawback is that, once your child comes of age at 18, he or she can demand that you hand over the money and assets in the trust. A further point to bear in mind is that, if your child were to die before reaching 18, the trust property would count as part of the child's estate and would be subject to the intestacy rules (see Chapter 12), since a minor is not able to make a valid will.

Gifts from friends and relatives

Income from a gift given by anyone other than a parent will count as the child's own income, so the child can set any unused personal allowance against it. You will need to be able to distinguish such gifts from those given by a parent. It would be sensible to invest the two types of gift separately: for example, small parental gifts in one building society account, gifts from other relatives and friends in another. And it is a good idea to ask people who give money or investments to your child to accompany them with a brief note stating the amount of the gift and who it is from. Keep such notes and letters in a safe place in case the Inland Revenue needs to see them.

Chapter 10

Using trusts

PLANNING FOR THE FUTURE

Ruth and David have become grandparents for the first time. 'I want to give the baby a nest egg for her future,' David explains to his solicitor. 'Of course, she's too young to handle money now, but I can put it in trust, can't I?'

'Yes, indeed,' replied the solicitor. 'You probably require what is known as an accumulation and maintenance trust. That would enable her to receive the money when she is adult, but gives the option to use it for her benefit in the meantime. Let us have a look at your precise circumstances and wishes.'

Trusts (which you may also come across as a form of 'settlement') are legal arrangements that enable you to give away assets but restrict or direct how and when they are used. Trusts can be used to make gifts in your lifetime and they can also be set up under the terms of a will. A trust involves three types of participant, as follows:

- *The settlor* This is the person who gives away the assets that are placed in the trust. A settlor can also be an organisation, and there might be more than one settlor of a trust. The settlor can also be a beneficiary and/or a trustee of the trust.
- *The beneficiary* This is a person who is to receive the assets or benefit from them. There will be rules about when and how the benefit is to be received. A beneficiary can also be an organisation – for example, a charity (see page 50) – and there can be, and often

is, more than one beneficiary of a trust. A beneficiary can also be a trustee and/or the settlor.

- *The trustee* This is the person – or, more usually, people – who looks after the assets, ensuring that they are invested and used in accordance with the rules of the trust and general trust law. Both settlors and beneficiaries may act as trustees, though often independent trustees will be chosen. A corporate trustee can be appointed, but for a family trust this would usually be disproportionately expensive.

So instead of making a gift outright, using a trust enables you (the settlor) to hand assets to a third party (the trustees) who will look after the assets and pass on the gift to the recipient (the beneficiary) in accordance with whatever rules or restrictions you – or the law – have stipulated. A trust can be a useful device in a wide range of circumstances. For example:

- *Giving to children* You want to make a gift to a child to be available to him or her when he or she is older.
- *Maintaining control* You might wish to give assets to someone who is not good at handling money, for example, someone with a careless financial record, or a person who is mentally infirm.
- *Giving to a group* You wish to give to a group of people that might not yet be complete, for example, you might want all your grandchildren, some of whom may not yet be born, to share a gift.
- *Separating income from capital* Useful where you wish to give assets to someone at some future time, but want someone else to have the use of, or income from, the assets in the meantime.
- *Giving on special occasions* You may want to make a gift only on the occasion of some possible, but indeterminate, event, such as a marriage or birth.
- *Maintaining confidentiality* You may want to arrange now to make a gift at some time in the future, but would prefer the beneficiary to be unaware of the gift at present.
- *Tax efficiency* Sometimes a gift into trust can save tax, or avoid tax problems, which you would incur if making an outright gift.

More about the participants

The settlor

As the settlor – i.e. the person making the gift to the trust – it is up to you to specify what you want the trust to do, who the beneficiaries are and what powers the trustees will have. In some respects, you are constrained by the laws concerning trusts. For example, the maximum lifetime of most trusts is 80 years and there are also restrictions on the maximum length of time over which income can be accumulated within a trust before being paid out to one or more beneficiaries. Many statutory rules – e.g. concerning the investments used by the trust – come into play only if the trust deed and rules for your particular trust do not specify some other approach. Provided a solicitor draws up the trust deed and rules for you, it is unlikely that you will fall foul of the legal requirements.

Watch out for the tax rules. Any income from the trust property will count as yours – and so be taxed as yours – if:

- you or your husband or wife can benefit from the trust either now or at some time in the future. This is called having a retained interest
- income or capital are paid out to, or for the benefit of, your child or children under the age of 18 (and unmarried). This is ignored if the income comes to no more than £100 a year per parent (see Chapter 9)
- you or your husband or wife enter into various loan and repayment arrangements with the trust.

The rules on retained interest do not apply simply if you are a named beneficiary of the trust – their impact is much wider. For example, if the trust says that your grandchild will become entitled to the trust property provided she reaches age 25 but you fail to say what happens if she does not reach that age, you will be deemed to be a potential beneficiary because if your grandchild were to die before age 25, the property would revert back to you, the settlor. Similarly, if the trustees had the power to give the trust property to any other trust which includes your grandchild as a beneficiary, you would be treated as having an interest because you could be a beneficiary too of some other trust to which the property could be given.

Note, too, that if you are both the settlor and a beneficiary under a trust, the reservation of benefit rules apply (see page 108). This means that when you die, the trust property will count as part of your estate which could create or increase an IHT bill. Similarly, if you cease to be a beneficiary under the trust, you will be treated as having made a gift at that time – the gift will count either as a PET (see page 104) or a chargeable gift (see page 98) depending on the type of trust involved.

Trustees

If you are a non-professional trustee, you are expected to carry out your role carefully and sensibly with about the same standard and skill that would be expected of a businessman or woman. As such, you need to make sure that you understand the nature of the trust and the duties required of you. Your first step must be to read the documents relating to the trust. You will have responsibilities in some or all of the following areas:

- *Investments* You should ensure that the trust fund is invested prudently and as allowed either by the trust deed or by the law. Where some beneficiaries have an interest in income, others in capital, you must strike a fair balance between their interests, so that you do not favour one group of beneficiaries over another. You must regularly review the investments to ensure that they are still appropriate and producing an acceptable return.
- *Accounts* You are required to draw up annual accounts, though usually there is no requirement to have them audited. Income beneficiaries can ask to see the full accounts and capital beneficiaries have a right on request to see accounts showing how the fund is invested. Although not required by law, it is good practice for trustees to provide beneficiaries with a copy automatically.
- *Payments to beneficiaries* You must ensure that payments are made at the right time to the appropriate beneficiaries. When a trust comes to an end, you should ask the beneficiaries to release you from your obligations as trustee on production of the final accounts, showing that the trust money has all been paid out
- *Discretionary powers* The trust deed will specify the extent to which the trustees are given any powers to decide, for example, who will

benefit, when they will benefit, how much they will receive and what changes can be made to any of these. You might need only to exercise such powers in certain specified circumstances or you could be required to review your decisions regularly. Unless the trust deed says differently, trustees are required to make unanimous decisions.

You are not allowed to profit from being a trustee, so you cannot claim any kind of fee, unless the trust deed specifically allows you to do so. You should ensure that there is no conflict of interest between your own affairs and your duties under the trust.

The beneficiaries

Depending on the way the trust is drawn up, as a beneficiary, you might have an interest in the income of the trust or its capital or both. Your entitlement could be outright or it might be dependent on some event – e.g. reaching a particular age or getting married.

If you are under the age of 18, the trust deed may allow for you to receive income or capital, or for trust money to be used for your benefit – e.g. paying school fees. (Though if your parents are the settlors, they should be aware that the income paid out – and, in some cases, the capital too – will generally be treated as their own income for tax purposes.) Any income which is not paid out is accumulated within the trust and, unless the trust deed says otherwise, the income beneficiaries become entitled to it on reaching age 18 (or getting married at an earlier age).

As a beneficiary, you can challenge (through the courts) the actions of the trustees if you believe they are not administering the trust properly or they are failing to look after the trust assets adequately. But you have no rights to alter the actions or decisions of the trustees if they have acted within their powers.

You can inspect the trust deed and rules and records of meetings, but not any records giving the reasons behind the decisions taken by the trustees when they have exercised their discretionary powers.

Choosing the appropriate trust

There are four types of trust: bare trusts, interest-in-possession trusts, discretionary trusts, and accumulation-and-maintenance trusts (which are in fact a special type of discretionary trust that benefits from favourable tax treatment as long as special rules are kept). Which type of trust will best suit your needs is dictated in part by the characteristics of each type of trust. Of great importance, however, is your tax position and the tax treatment of the different trusts.

The tax treatment of trusts is undoubtedly complex and there are numerous pitfalls for the unwary. The wording of the trust deed and the powers of the trustees can be crucial in assessing which tax regime applies. You are strongly advised to take advice from a solicitor before deciding on whether or not to use a trust and which type would be appropriate, and you should ask a solicitor to draw up the trust deed.[23]

The main types of trust

Bare trust

How does it work

This is the simplest type of trust, requiring very little administration. Someone holds assets as nominee for someone else – most commonly, a parent or some other relative holds investments given by the parent to their child as outlined in Chapter 9. Property is transferred to the bare trustee who holds it for the beneficiary and uses it in accordance with his or her instructions. So provided the beneficiary is aged 18 or more (or is married if younger), he or she can call for the income and/or capital at any time and the trustee has no right to withhold it. For tax purposes, the beneficiary – not the trustee – is treated as the owner of the trust property.

Pros and cons

A bare trust is not a complex trust to administer. Tax on the trust property will generally be lower than if it were held in, say, an accumulation-and-maintenance trust. Watch out if you are a parent making a gift to your child to be held in a bare trust. Income from any gifts made on or after 9 March 1999 is taxed as yours, not the

---

[23]In the book and will kit mentioned on page 165, some of the pro forma wills provided include clauses for setting up trusts. Use these only if you are certain that the pro forma will selected reflects your wishes. If in doubt, consult a solicitor. Never try to adapt the wording of one of these wills if it does not quite match your circumstances.

child's, unless it comes to no more than £100 – see Chapter 9. Income from gifts from other sources – for example, from grandparents – counts as that of the child. And any capital gains, whatever the source of the investments, are taxed as the child's. This can make a bare trust more tax-efficient than other trust options in suitable cases. Against this, you must balance the drawbacks. Once the trust is set up, you cannot change the beneficiaries or the shares in which they own the trust property. The settlor has no control at all over the use of the trust property once the child has reached his or her majority. The trust property is part of the beneficiary's estate when he or she dies – if the beneficiary is under the age of 18 at the time of death, he or she would die intestate (see Chapter 12) since he or she would be too young to have made a will.

Possible uses

* Making a gift of property to a child – e.g. a share in a family business – which the child does not yet have the legal capacity to hold because of his or her young age.
* Building up a nest egg for a child to have on reaching age 18.

EXAMPLE 10.1

In 1998 Michael (see Chapter 9) decided to give Rebecca another £10,000, but to put it into a bare trust. Michael's sister, Nichola, took on the role of trustee and the £10,000 was invested in her name in a selection of deposits and corporate bonds. Provided the income was reinvested in the trust and neither used for Rebecca's benefit nor paid out to her, it did not count as Michael's income and so he paid no tax on it. The income was treated as Rebecca's but she did not pay tax on it either because it fell within her personal allowance. Fortunately the 1999 Budget changes affect only bare trusts being newly set up or new funds being added to existing trusts, so the income continues to be treated as Rebecca's and thus escapes tax.

Interest-in-possession trust

Also known as a 'life-interest trust' and a type of 'fixed-interest trust'.

How does it work?

One or more beneficiaries have the right to receive income earned by the assets in the trust as that income arises, or alternatively have the right to use the assets held by the trust, for example, the right to live in a house. Eventually – for example, on the death of the life interest beneficiaries, or at a given date, or when a specified event, such as marriage, occurs – the assets in the trust are distributed. The person or people who receive the assets are said to hold the 'reversionary interest'. The beneficiaries who receive the income (or use of the assets) need not be the same as the beneficiaries who have the reversionary interest, though they could be. For example, you might specify in your will that your share of the family home be put into trust, giving your husband or wife a life interest so that he or she could continue living there as long as desired, but giving the reversionary interest to your children so that they would inherit on the death of your spouse. See also Example 10.2.

Pros and cons

Interest-in-possession trusts are not as flexible as discretionary trusts or accumulation-and-maintenance trusts. Nevertheless, they have been popular in the past particularly because they enjoyed more advantageous CGT treatment than other types of trust. But, from 6 April 1998, the CGT treatment of interest-in-possession trusts has been brought into line with the tax treatment of other types of trust – see page 135.

Possible uses

- Where you eventually want to pass on assets to one or more people but need to provide for someone else in the interim – see Example 10.2.
- Where you do not want the beneficiary to have full control of the assets in the trust, or you want to defer handing over control until a later date.

- Because the capital gains tax treatment used to be more favourable than the regime applying to discretionary trusts, an interest-in-possession trust was often the best choice if you wanted to give to adults. But from 6 April 1998 this advantage no longer applies (see page 135). You should also be wary if you might want to alter the people who benefit from the trust income or the shares the beneficiaries have in it – such alterations will usually count as gifts from one beneficiary to another under the IHT rules.
- If you want to give to children, usually an accumulation-and-maintenance trust would be a better choice. However, you could adapt an interest-in-possession trust to suit gifts to children by, for example, specifying that income should be held for the child(ren) until they reach age 18. In effect, this is combining a bare trust (see page 126) with the interest-in-possession trust.

EXAMPLE 10.2

David's will stipulates that, on his death, a large part of his assets should be placed in trust. The trustees would invest the assets as they saw fit and the income from them (and use of his former share of the family home) should go to his wife during her lifetime. On his wife's death, the assets are to be shared equally between their three children. David has drawn up his will in this way, first, to guard against his widow being short of money during her lifetime and, secondly, to ensure that his children will eventually receive his assets even if his widow remarries.

Discretionary trust

How does it work?

If a trust is not a bare trust or an interest-in-possession trust, then it is by default a discretionary trust. That said, the distinguishing features are usually that income can be accumulated within the trust to be paid out later or to be paid out at the discretion of the trustees and that there is usually more than one beneficiary. Often there will be a 'class' of beneficiaries, such as your children or your grandchildren, not all of whom have to be born at the time the trust is set up.

Pros and cons

Although discretionary trusts are very flexible, they are treated less favourably for tax purposes than either interest-in-possession trusts or accumulation-and-maintenance trusts.

Possible uses

- Where you want to be able to alter the people (or bodies) who will benefit under the trust.
- Where you want to be able to alter the proportions in which the beneficiaries share in income and/or capital from the trust.

EXAMPLE 10.3

John had been ill for some time and, knowing that he did not have long to live, he checked his will and brought it up to date. He was a widower and had six sons whose ages ranged from 22 to 30. Two of the sons had good, secure incomes, while three had not settled down to careers yet but had only minor financial problems. However, the other son was generally in financial difficulties – largely of his own making.

John wanted to be fair to all his boys, but was not happy with the idea of just sharing out his assets between them. They did not all have the same need, and the youngest son in particular would be likely to squander any inheritance. John wanted a solution which would ensure that help was available to all his sons if they needed it but would protect the assets otherwise. He decided to set up a discretionary trust in favour of all the sons. He appointed his own two brothers (the sons' uncles) as trustees and gave them discretion to make payments and loans from the trust fund to the sons if or when, in the trustees' opinion, such help was warranted. After ten years (by which time John felt the boys should all take responsibility for themselves), the remaining trust assets were to be distributed equally among them.

Accumulation-and-maintenance trust

How does it work?

This is a special type of discretionary trust but, provided certain rules are kept, it escapes the worst of the unfavourable tax treatment normally applying to discretionary trusts. The rules include:

- one or more of the beneficiaries must become entitled to either the income or capital from the trust on or before reaching age 25
- in the run-up to the entitlement above coming into effect, no beneficiary can have an interest in possession. Instead, income from the assets in the trust must be accumulated, except that it can be used to pay for the maintenance, education or other benefit of one or more of the beneficiaries
- the trust can exist for a maximum of 25 years, unless all the beneficiaries have a common grandparent, in which case, the life of the trust can be longer (adopted children and stepchildren are treated in the same way as other children of a family for the purpose of this test)
- although the beneficiaries can be a group, such as all your grandchildren, there must be at least one member of the group living at the time the trust is set up. (However, if there is just one member and that person dies before any others are born, the trust can continue.)

Pros and cons
The accumulation-and-maintenance trust is flexible and tax-efficient, but only for gifts to children. Unlike a direct gift or a bare trust (see page 126), the trust property is not part of a beneficiary's estate if he or she dies.

Possible uses

- Where you want to be able to alter the people who will benefit under the trust, e.g. by allowing for children who are as yet unborn.
- Where you want to be able to alter the proportions in which the beneficiaries share in income and/or capital from the trust.
- Where you want to make gifts as a parent to your child(ren) without income from the gift being treated as yours (see Chapter 9).
- Building up a nest egg for children, grandchildren, etc.
- Paying school fees.

EXAMPLE 10.4

David set up a trust to accept a gift for his first granddaughter, Jemima. Bearing in mind that there might be more grandchildren to come, he established an accumulation-and-maintenance trust in favour of all his grandchildren. For the present, he has settled £6,000 in the trust, but can add more later if he wishes. Jemima is to become entitled to a lump sum from the trust when she reaches age 21. In the meantime, money can be paid out – to pay for school fees, say – at the discretion of the trustees, who are David and his wife, Ruth.

Other special types of trust

Accumulation-and-maintenance trusts are just one type of discretionary trust which qualifies for special treatment. There are others. Most are outside the scope of gift planning (they include, *inter alia*, pension schemes, personal pension plans, compensation funds and unit trusts), but two may be of use:

- *charitable trusts* If you want to give large amounts to a range of charities, setting up your own charitable trust is an option worth considering (see page 51)
- *disabled trusts* For assets placed in trust on or after 10 March 1981, mainly for the benefit of someone who is incapable of looking after their own property because of mental disorder, or someone who is receiving attendance allowance, the disabled person is treated as if he or she has an interest in possession. This means that the interest-in-possession tax rules apply rather than those for discretionary trusts (see below).

A special type of interest-in-possession trust can also be useful if you want to make a gift to someone, but you have real doubts about whether he or she can be trusted to act responsibly. This is a 'protective trust'. Basically, the beneficiary is entitled to the income from, or use of, the trust assets for as long as he or she behaves responsibly. But, if a specified event occurs – for example, the beneficiary becomes bankrupt – the interest in possession ceases. The trust automatically converts into a discretionary trust and the trustees decide how best to use the assets for the maintenance and support of the original beneficiary and/or his or her family.

Taxation of trusts

The tax treatment of trusts is crucial to any decision regarding the use of a trust as a way of making gifts. Unfortunately, it is also complex. Back in 1991, the government proposed changes to simplify the income and capital taxation of trusts and to bring it into harmony with the personal tax regime.[24] These proposals were abandoned but then partially re-introduced in the 1995 Finance Act. Further tinkering has been made in both the 1998 and 1999 Budgets, but the income tax treatment of trusts, in particular, remains detailed and complex. The IHT position of trusts was overhauled fairly recently, but could be altered further if the Labour government decides at some future date to make substantial changes to the IHT regime.

Bare trusts

Putting a gift into trust

Your gift into a bare trust counts as a potentially exempt transfer (PET), so there is no IHT to pay provided you survive for at least seven years – see page 104. No special rules apply regarding CGT – check the ordinary rules in Chapters 6 and 7 to see if any CGT will be payable.

The trust's tax position

The trust does not have a separate tax identity from the beneficiary. Income and gains from the trust property are treated in the same way as if the property were owned directly by the beneficiary. This means that income is taxed at the beneficiary's top rate after taking into account allowances and any other deductions. The exception to this is where the assets in the trust are a gift from a parent to an unmarried child under age 18 and the gift was made on or after 9 March 1999. If such income exceeds £100, it is treated as that of the parent. This applies whether the income is accumulated or paid out. See Chapter 9 for further details.

---

[24] Inland Revenue *Trusts: a consultative document*, London, Inland Revenue, 1991.

Gains are taxed at the beneficiary's top rate after taking account of the yearly tax-free slice.

Payments to beneficiaries

Any tax has already been paid as income and gains arose – see above. There is no further tax to pay when payments are made to the beneficiary or used for their benefit.

The exception is where the assets in the trust are a gift from a parent to an unmarried child under age 18 and the gift was made before 9 March 1999. In this case, provided income was accumulated within the trust it will have been treated as that of the child. But once paid out to the child, or used for the child's benefit, it becomes taxable as that of the parent if the income exceeds £100. See Chapter 9 for further details.

When the bare trust ends

The trust property has been treated as owned by the beneficiary throughout, therefore there is no change when the beneficiary takes outright possession of the the trust property.

EXAMPLE 10.5

Rebecca is the beneficiary of a bare trust containing £10,000 capital. This was a gift from her father made before 9 March 1999. The capital has earned approximately £1,000 a year income and a small amount of capital profit. Both are well within Rebecca's 1999–2000 tax allowances of £4,335 personal allowance against taxable income and £7,100 against chargeable gains. On reaching the age of 18, Rebecca intends to ask the trustee, Aunt Nichola, to carry on acting as trustee but to advance Rebecca a regular income to support her while she is at university — this will be taxed in the same way as if it had been accumulated within the trust. On finishing her university course, Rebecca intends to take outright possession of the trust property; this will not give rise to any tax charge.

Interest-in-possession trusts

Putting a gift into trust

If you make a gift which is placed in an interest-in-possession trust, you are treated as if you had made a potentially exempt transfer (PET). No IHT is charged provided you survive for seven years after making the gift (see page 104 for more details). If you die within seven years, the trustees will normally be liable for the tax due. No special rules apply in respect of CGT, so check the ordinary rules to see if tax will be payable (see Chapters 6 and 7).

The trust's tax position

Income from the assets in the trust may be paid either direct to the beneficiaries or first to the trustees who then pass it on to the beneficiaries.

The trustees are responsible for tax on income earned by the trust assets. Tax may be payable at any of three rates, depending on the type of income involved (rates apply to 1999-2000):

- on dividends, distributions from share-based unit trusts and similar investments, the rate is 10 per cent
- on interest income (for example, interest from savings accounts, corporate bonds or unit trusts investing in bonds), tax is charged at the savings rate of 20 per cent
- on any other income, tax is charged at the basic rate which is 23 per cent.

Example 10.6 shows how this can work out in practice.

Until 5 April 1998, an interest-in-possession trust was also liable for CGT on any capital gains only at the basic rate. No further CGT is payable if capital is paid out to a beneficiary. Therefore, the low rate of CGT on the trust's gains made this form of trust particularly attractive where a beneficiary was a higher-rate taxpayer (who would normally be taxed on gains at a rate of 40 per cent). The government, worried that interest-in-possession trusts were being set up purely for tax-avoidance reasons, closed the loophole. From 6 April 1998 onwards, interest-in-possession trusts were brought into line with discretionary trusts (including accumulation-and-maintenance trusts): gains realised by all these trusts are now taxable at a uniform special trust rate of 34 per cent. The first slice of gains each tax year is tax-free. The tax-free slice for a trust is set at half the rate for an individual – i.e. £3,550 in 1999–2000.

Payments to beneficiaries

Income paid out to beneficiaries is broadly treated as if it had been received directly by them. This means three different treatments may apply, depending on the type of income:

- dividends and similar income are received net of tax at 10 per cent and accompanied by a tax credit. From 6 April 1999 onwards, non-taxpayers cannot reclaim this tax credit. Lower- and basic-rate taxpayers have no further tax to pay. Higher-rate taxpayers must pay further tax on the grossed-up amount of the dividend – see Example 10.7
- interest income is paid net of tax at 20 per cent. Non-taxpayers can reclaim this. Lower-rate taxpayers cannot reclaim any of the tax deducted. Basic-rate taxpayers have no further tax to pay. Higher-rate taxpayers must pay extra on the grossed-up amount of the interest – see Example 10.7
- all other income is paid with tax at the basic rate already deducted. Non-taxpayers and lower-rate taxpayers can reclaim all or part of this. Higher-rate taxpayers have extra to pay – see Example 10.7

There may be arrangements for beneficiaries to receive income direct from the trust investments instead of the income passing through the hands of the trustees. In this case, the beneficiary accounts for tax direct to the Inland Revenue.

If you receive payment of capital from the trust, there is no CGT for you to pay and you cannot reclaim any CGT paid by the trust.

When the interest in possession ends

If you have an interest in possession, you are treated, for tax purposes, as owning the assets in the trust – the reversionary interest is ignored. If there is more than one beneficiary, you are treated as owning the trust assets in proportion to your shares in the income from them. When your interest in possession ends, you are deemed to make a gift of the assets to the beneficiary with the reversionary interest. Provided you are 'giving' the assets to an individual or to an appropriate type of trust, the gift counts as a PET and no tax is payable as long as you survive for seven years (see page 104). If the assets pass, say, to a discretionary trust, the gift counts as chargeable and there may be an immediate IHT bill, depending on your running total of gifts during the last seven years (see page 98).

If, when the trust ends, you become entitled to receive the trust property outright, there is no IHT liability.

If a beneficiary's interest in possession ends during his or her lifetime, the beneficiary is deemed to be disposing of the trust assets and there may be CGT to pay. There is no CGT liability when a life interest ends on the death of the beneficiary holding the interest.

A reversionary interest in an interest-in-possession trust counts as 'excluded property' for IHT purposes, which means that it is completely outside the IHT net. This can be useful, since a gift of a reversionary interest cannot create an IHT bill (see Example 10.8).

EXAMPLE 10.6

Molly was left a life interest in a trust set up by her husband, Charlie, who died several years ago. The trust holds a mix of investments, some property and various shares and bonds. In 1999-2000, the income and tax position of the trust was as follows:

Income

Income from property (received gross – i.e. no tax deducted)	£4,000
Dividends from shares (net of 10% tax credit)	£1,800
Interest income (net of 20% savings tax)	£3,200

Tax

Tax at 23% on property income (23% x £4,000)	£ 920
Tax at 10% already deducted from dividends (10/90 x £1,800)	£ 200
Tax at 20% already deducted from interest (20/80 x £3,200)	£ 800
Total tax paid	£1,920
Income after tax (£4,000 – £920 + £1,800 + £3,200)	£8,080

EXAMPLE 10.7

All the income from the trust in Example 10.6 is paid out to Molly in 1999-2000. Molly has income from other sources too and is a higher-rate taxpayer. Her trust income is treated for tax as follows:

Income from property Molly receives £3,080 from which tax at 23 per cent has already been deducted. She grosses this up by doing the following sum: 100/77 x £3,080 = £4,000. Higher-rate tax on this is 40% x £4,000 = £1,600 but tax of £920 has already been paid, so Molly must now pay £1,600 − £920 = £680

Income from shares Molly receives £1,800 in dividends plus a tax credit for £200. She grosses up the dividends by doing the following sum: 100/90 x £1,800 = £2,000. Higher-rate tax on this is 32.5% x £2,000 = £650 but tax of £200 has already been paid, so Molly must now pay £650 − £200 = £450

Interest income Molly receives £3,200 from which tax at 20 per cent has already been deducted. She grosses this up by doing the following sum: 100/80 x £3,200 = £4,000. Higher-rate tax on this is 40% x £4,000 = £1,600 but tax of £800 has already been paid, so Molly must now pay £1,600 − £800 = £800.

In total, Molly has further tax of £680 + £450 + £800 = £1,930 to pay on her trust income. This leaves her with a net sum of £8,080 − £1,930 = £6,150.

EXAMPLE 10.8

When Charlie died, he left part of his assets (some £100,000 in total) in trust, giving his wife, Molly, a life interest in the income from the trust and his daughter, Pru, the reversionary interest in the trust property. Pru is in her thirties and has children of her own. Her husband has a well-paid job and the family is financially comfortable. Pru would prefer that her father's assets passed to her children. So she decides to release her reversionary interest in the trust and give it to the children. There is no IHT to pay, because reversionary interests are excluded from the IHT regime.

Discretionary trusts

Putting a gift into trust

A gift put into a discretionary trust counts as a chargeable gift for IHT and can create an immediate tax bill (see page 98). Whether or not you have to pay any tax depends on whether you can claim an exemption (for example, the yearly tax-free slice of £3,000) or, if not, on your running total of chargeable gifts during the previous seven years. If the gift when added to your running total is less than your tax-free slice (£231,000 in 1999–2000), there will be no immediate IHT bill.

Note that, if you set up other trusts on the same day, they can mean the trust has to pay extra IHT later on – see below. Try to avoid setting up other trusts on the same day as a discretionary trust.

CGT may be due on the gift, if you are giving assets other than cash, but you can claim hold-over relief (see page 91).

The trust's tax position

There is a 'periodic charge' for IHT on the value of the trust property. This charge is made on the tenth anniversary of the setting-up of the trust and at ten-year intervals after that. The amount of tax due is worked out as follows:

- *Add* up the value of the trust at the time of the tax charge *and* any gifts made by the settlor (i.e. the person who set up the discretionary trust) to other trusts (apart from charitable trusts) set up on the same day at their value on that day. To this, *add* the value of chargeable gifts made by the settlor in the seven years up to the date of the trust starting.
- Work out the tax due on that total amount by *deducting* the tax-free slice and *multiplying* by 20 per cent (in the 1999–2000 tax year).
- *Divide* the tax due by the value of everything owned by the discretionary trust. This gives you the 'effective rate of tax'.
- Take 30 per cent of the effective rate (i.e. *multiply* by 0.3). This gives you the rate at which tax will be charged on the trust property.

This means that the *highest* rate of tax that will have to be paid is 30 per cent of the lifetime rate of 20 per cent – that is, 6 per cent – and the rate could be as low as nothing at all.

If money or assets are paid out of a discretionary trust, an 'interim charge' for IHT is made and must be paid by the trustees. The charge is worked out by multiplying the full ten-year charges by 1/40 for each three-month period during which the property was in the trust since the last periodic charge to IHT. (The procedure is slightly different for payments made before the first ten-year period is up.) This interim charge is also called an 'exit charge'. The tax charge is scaled down similarly in the case of property added to the trust after the start of the relevant ten-year period.

EXAMPLE 10.9

Peter set up a discretionary trust on 1 May 1989, paying £60,000 into it. That day, he also set up an interest-in-possession trust in favour of his daughter and paid £50,000 into that. His cumulative total of chargeable gifts over the seven years before 1 May 1989 was £20,000.

On 1 January 1998, the first ten-year IHT charge becomes payable on the discretionary trust, which is now valued at £180,000. The tax due is worked out as follows:

Current value of discretionary trust	£180,000
plus original value of other trust set up on 1 May 1989	£50,000
plus Peter's seven-year running total up to 30 April 1989	£20,000
	£250,000
less tax-free slice	£231,000
	£19,000
Tax @ 20% on £19,000	£3,800
Effective rate of tax (£3,800 ÷ £180,000)	2.1%
30% x effective rate	0.06%
IHT due on the trust (0.06% x £180,000)	£1,140

The trustees are also responsible for paying income tax on any income received by the trust. This is paid at one of two rates, depending on the type of income involved (rates are for 1999-2000):

- on dividends from shares, distributions from share-based unit trusts and similar investments, tax is paid at a rate of 25 per cent
- on other income, tax is paid at 34 per cent.

Example 10.10 shows how this can work in practice. These rates are higher than those levied on income from interest-in-possession trusts – see page 135. The reason for this is that beneficiaries of discretionary trusts might have a wide variety of personal tax positions. The tax rates applicable to the discretionary trust are supposed to strike a balance between the basic and higher rates of tax which might apply to beneficiaries.

From 6 April 1999 onwards, trustees must effectively account for extra tax when they pay out income to beneficiaries. This is because the trustees can no longer count the tax credit on dividends the trust has received as part of the tax it deducts from payments to beneficiaries (see below). Where a trust has accumulated funds or other income out of which to pay this extra tax, it might still pass on the full after-tax amount of dividend income. But a trust without alternative funds will be forced to reduce the amount of dividend income it can pass on to beneficiaries. See Example 10.11.

CGT on any taxable capital gains is also payable by the trustees at 34 per cent, though the trust can set a tax-free allowance (£3,550 in 1999–2000) against the first slice of gains.

Payments to beneficiaries

Unlike an interest-in-possession trust (see page 136), income paid out from a discretionary trust is treated in just one way, regardless of the source of income. It is all paid out with tax at a rate of 34 per cent already deducted. As a beneficiary, you receive the net income plus a 34 per cent tax credit. The sum of the two counts as gross income which is taxable but you set the tax credit against your tax bill. In this way, you will normally receive a tax refund if your top rate of tax is lower than 34 per cent. Higher-rate taxpayers have extra tax to pay.

On the face of it, you might think that this opens up a way of reclaiming tax on dividends and similar income from April 1999 onwards (when such tax generally ceased to be reclaimable). In practice, this is not the case. As outlined above, from April 1999 onwards, the trustees must effectively pay extra tax when income is distributed. This means that, unless the trust has other funds available to meet the tax bill, it can afford to pass on to beneficiaries less of the dividend income it receives. So indirectly, you do feel the impact of tax on dividends ceasing to be reclaimable.

If you receive a payment of capital from the trust, there is no CGT for you to pay and you cannot reclaim any CGT paid by the trust. Note that once income has been accumulated within the trust, the payment of it to a beneficiary will normally count as a payment of capital.

When the trust ends

When the discretionary trust comes to an end, an 'exit' charge is made on the whole of the trust property as if it were any other payment from the trust (see above).

EXAMPLE 10.10

Some years ago, Jaspar and Anne set up a discretionary trust in favour of their grandchildren. The trust holds a mix of investments, some property and various shares and bonds. In 1999-2000, the income and tax position of the trust (before making any payments to beneficiaries) was as follows:

Income

Income from property (received gross – i.e. no tax deducted)	£4,000
Dividends from shares (net of 10% tax credit)	£1,800
Interest income (net of 20% savings tax)	£3,200

Tax

Tax at 34% on property income (34% x £4,000)	£1,360
Tax at 10% already deducted from dividends (10/90 x £1,800)	£200
Additional tax on dividends: 25% of grossed-up amount (100/90 x £1,800 = £2,000) less £200 already paid	£300
Tax at 20% already deducted from interest (20/80 x £3,200)	£800
Additional tax on interest: 34% of grossed-up amount (100/80 x £3,200 = £4,000) less £800 already paid	£560
Total tax paid	£3,220
Income after tax (£4,000 – £1,360 + £1,800 – £300 + £3,200 – £560)	£6,780

EXAMPLE 10.11

The trust in Example 10.10 generally passes the whole of its dividend income each year to one of the beneficiaries. The position in 1998-9 and 1999-2000 is set out below.

1998-9

Dividend income received by the trust	£1,800
Reclaimable tax credit at 20%	£450
Additional tax due on dividends: 34% of grossed-up dividend	
(100/80 x £1,800 = £2,000) less £450 already paid	£315
Dividend available for distribution (£1,800 – £315)	£1,485
Tax credit accompanying dividend distribution	
(34/66 x £1,485)	£765
Against which trust can set tax paid	£315
And tax credit	£450
Additional tax payable by trust on distribution to beneficiary	£0

1999-2000

Dividend income received by the trust	£1,800
Non-reclaimable tax credit at 10%	£200
Additional tax due on dividends: 25% of grossed-up dividend	
(100/90 x £1,800 = £2,000) less £200 already paid	£300
Dividend available for distribution (£1,800 – £300)	£1,500
Tax credit accompanying dividend distribution	
(34/66 x £1,500)	£772.73
Against which trust can set tax paid	£300
But not non-reclaimable tax credit of £200	
Additional tax payable by trust on distribution to beneficiary	£472.73

If the trustees do not wish to use other funds to meet the £472.73 additional tax bill, they must reduce the amount of dividend which they pass on to the beneficiary.

Accumulation-and-maintenance trusts

Putting a gift into trust

Although accumulation-and-maintenance trusts are a special form of discretionary trust, the tax rules are much more favourable. A payment into an accumulation-and-maintenance trust counts as a PET (see page 104) and so there is no tax to pay provided you survive for seven years after making the gift.

Normal CGT rules apply to a gift to an accumulation-and-maintenance trust, so you will need to check whether there is any CGT to pay (see Chapters 6 and 7).

The trust's tax position

An accumulation-and-maintenance trust is not subject to the periodic charge regime – that is, there is no IHT to pay on the value of the trust during the lifetime of the trust nor is there any IHT charge when payments are made to beneficiaries.

The income and capital gains tax position of the trust is the same as for other discretionary trusts – see above.

Payments to beneficiaries

The rules are the same as for other discretionary trusts (see page 141).

Bear in mind that, if you set up an accumulation-and-maintenance trust for your own child, any income paid out to your child under the age of 18 (and unmarried) or used for his or her benefit will count as your income for tax purposes. Any capital paid out will be treated in the same way to the extent that it can be matched against income accumulated within the trust. But you can avoid income being taxed as yours if you leave all the income and capital to accumulate within the trust.

When the trust ends

There is no IHT charge. The trustees may need to pay CGT on any capital gains – this cannot be reclaimed by the beneficiaries. Amounts received by beneficiaries are treated as under 'Payments to beneficiaries' on page 141.

Table 10.1 Which type of trust?

	Bare Trust	Interest-in-possession	Discretionary	Accumulation-and-maintenance
IHT status of gift when trust set up	PET	PET	Chargeable gift	PET
IHT regime once trust up and running	Does not apply	Favourable	Unfavourable	Favourable
Trust pays tax on income at:[†]	Beneficiary's own rate	23%, 20% and 10%	34% and 25%	34% and 25%
Trust pays tax on gains at:[†]	Beneficiary's own rate	34%	34%	34%
Can build up income within trust	Yes	Not usually	Yes	Yes
Can easily alter who benefits	No	No for income, yes for capital	Yes	Yes
Can easily alter the shares of the beneficiaries	No	No for income, yes for capital	Yes	Yes
Other				Only for minors

[†]1999–2000 rates.

Chapter 11

Lifetime gift planning

SKIP THE COUNTRY

'I'd like to give Jake the paddock. The trouble is now that the local council has included it in the development plan, it's worth such a lot. I'll have a massive capital gains tax bill to pay,' groaned Patrick. 'There's only one thing for it,' soothed his wife, Jenny. 'We'll have to flee the country – become tax exiles. But we'll have to stay away for at least five years.' 'Jenny, you're up to something . . .' Patrick had belatedly spied the stack of travel brochures.

If you want to make gifts during your lifetime, most will be free of IHT either because of some specific exemption or because they count as PETs (and so are tax-free provided you survive for seven years). Therefore your main concern is how to give without triggering an unnecessary CGT bill or creating income tax problems. Following the tips in this chapter can help, but if your affairs are complex it is advisable to get help from an accountant. (See Addresses at the back of the book.)

Give exempt assets

If you can, give away things which are outside the scope of CGT – for example, cash or personal items worth less than £6,000 – see Chapter 6.

Use your tax-free slice

If you are planning to make a gift within the next few years and it's showing a fairly sizeable gain on which you would face a hefty CGT bill, consider making use of your tax-free slice between now and the year in which you make the gift. You can dispose of a certain amount of chargeable assets, which would otherwise be taxable, each year without having to pay CGT – the tax-free slice for 1999–2000 is £7,100.

New-style bed and breakfast

Instead of wasting your CGT tax-free slice in years when you are not making any gifts (or other disposals), a widely used ploy used to be to sell assets, most commonly shares, and buy them back again the next day – a practice called 'bed-and-breakfasting'. This realised the gain (or loss) on the asset for tax purposes, using up your tax-free slice for the year (or providing a loss to offset against other gains) and gave a new, higher initial value for calculating future gains on the asset.

However, the 1998 Budget brought traditional bed-and-breakfasting to an abrupt end. From 17 March 1998 onwards, any shares or similar assets which are sold and repurchased within a 30-day period are matched and any gain or loss which would otherwise have been realised is ignored for CGT purposes.

You could still bed-and-breakfast in the old way, but leaving more than 30 days between the sale and repurchase. However, this would be a high-risk strategy, since the stockmarket could move dramatically over a month. Alternative ways to realise gains or losses while keeping your assets largely unchanged include:

- 'bed-and-ISA' your shares. This means selling the shares and immediately buying them back within the shelter of an Individual Savings Account (ISA). An ISA must be taken out through an approved ISA manager (e.g. a stockbroker)
- if you are married, sell your shares and ask your husband or wife to buy the same shares immediately. Ownership has changed but at least the shares are still in the family
- sell your shares and simultaneously buy a call traded option which gives you the right to buy the same company's shares at a fixed

price on or before a set future date. This is a relatively expensive exercise because you must pay a premium for the option

- sell the shares in one company and buy back shares in another company which is expected to perform in a similar manner – usually shares in a company of similar size in the same sector. Deciding which shares are reasonably well-matched could be tricky.

Before attempting new-style bed-and-breakfasting, you would be wise to discuss the various possibilities with a stockbroker.

Use your husband's or wife's tax-free slice

If your husband or wife does not use his/her tax-free slice (£7,100 in 1999–2000) and you have a gift to make on which there is a sizeable gain, you might be able to reduce the CGT bill by first giving part or all of the asset to your husband or wife. Gifts between husband and wife are normally tax-free (see page 63). Note, however, that the gift to your husband or wife must be genuine and you cannot attach any conditions – e.g. insisting that he or she gives away the asset subsequently in accordance with your wishes. Therefore you need to be confident that you and your husband or wife have genuinely similar views and aspirations about making gifts to the recipient.

Skip the country?

In the past, CGT was payable only if you were resident and/or ordinarily resident in the UK during the tax year in which you realise a chargeable gain. However, following changes in the 1998 Budget, you can now still end up with a CGT bill even if you are living abroad.

For anyone who ceases to be resident from 17 March 1998 onwards and for anyone who becomes UK resident again from 6 April 1998 onwards, any gifts or other disposals he/she makes while abroad will be free of CGT only if he/she has been not resident and not ordinarily resident in the UK for five complete tax years or more.

Where your period abroad comes to less than five complete tax years, gains realised in the tax year in which you leave the UK will be taxable in that year. Gains realised while abroad will be taxed in the tax year of your return.

The tax statutes say very little about what the terms 'resident' and 'ordinarily resident' mean, but a body of case law has grown up. You will always count as resident for a tax year if you spend 183 days or more in the UK during the tax year, and if you spend fewer days there, you may still count as resident. You will usually count as 'ordinarily resident' if you live in the UK year after year, even if you are away temporarily. The main way in which someone who normally lives in the UK can count as not resident and not ordinarily resident is to go and work full-time abroad, provided the following conditions are met:

- your absence from the UK and your contract of employment both last at least a whole tax year
- you can make visits back home (e.g. for holidays) but the time spent in the UK must not add up to more than 183 days in any one tax year and, over the whole period abroad, must average only 91 days per tax year or less.

By concession, a husband or wife accompanying their spouse while he or she works abroad can also count as resident or non-resident. For more information about residency status, see Inland Revenue booklet IR20, *Residents and non-residents*, available from tax offices.★

Taking a decision to work abroad just so that you can avoid CGT may seem a drastic step. But, looked at from another perspective, if you do find yourself doing a stint working overseas, it would be an excellent time to consider making any gifts which could give rise to a large CGT bill.

EXAMPLE 11.1

Jenny is a fashion designer, working for an international firm. Usually, she is based in London, but in March 1999 she is posted to the USA. Her husband Patrick decides to go with her. The posting is due to last for a minimum of two years but can be extended thereafter on an annual basis. Jenny will have nine weeks' holiday a year when she can make visits back home. Provided Jenny continues to work abroad for at least five years, this would be an ideal opportunity to give their son, Jake, a piece of land which Patrick owns. The former paddock has been given development land status in the council's local plan which has boosted its value from a few thousand pounds to £150,000. Despite its high value, there is no CGT to pay on the gift, provided Jenny remains non-resident and not ordinarily resident for five whole tax years.

Don't forget hold-over relief

Hold-over relief (see page 9) lets you, in effect, give away your CGT bill along with the asset which is the subject of your gift. One of the circumstances in which you can claim hold-over relief is where the gift counts as a chargeable transfer for IHT. Making your gift to a discretionary trust would fit the bill. Provided you make sure that the gift is covered by one of the IHT exemptions (see Chapter 6) or falls within your tax-free slice (£231,000 for 1999–2000), there will be no IHT on the gift. However, make sure that a gift into trust suits your intentions and that you fully understand the tax position of the trust (see Chapter 10). It would be prudent to get advice from a solicitor.★

Gifts to children

It is difficult for a parent to make a gift to his/her child without income paid to the child or used for the benefit of the child counting as the parent's income for tax purposes (see Chapter 9). Ways to avoid this are:

- ensure such income comes to no more than £100 a year
- invest such gifts in tax-free investments, such as National Savings Children's Bonus Bonds and friendly society plans
- ensure that outright gifts are invested for capital gain, not income
- put the gift into an accumulation-and-maintenance trust (or any other type of trust) and allow income and gains to accumulate until the child reaches at least age 18 (or marries at an earlier age).

This problem affects only gifts from parents, so encourage other relatives to make gifts to your children. But beware of arrangements where a gift is made to your child in return for your making a reciprocal gift to someone else – such an arrangement is likely to fall foul of anti-avoidance rules. If the tax authorities reckon that the main aim of the arrangement is to avoid tax, they can disregard it and tax you on your child's income anyway.

Part 3

Inheritance

Whether you are writing your own will or sorting out someone else's will, please note that it is important to consult a legal adviser if substantial sums of money are involved and/or the situation is at all complex.

Chapter 12

Making a will

WILLS ARE IMPORTANT

'Now, Mr Hope' – the solicitor's face became more serious – 'I take it you have made a will?'

'Well, no,' replied Richard, 'but my affairs are very straightforward. Everything would go to my wife – after all, she'd have the children to look after.'

'Precisely, Mr Hope. Without a will, only part of your estate would pass to your wife. Although your children would also benefit, I'm afraid your wife might need to sell the home and there would certainly be a number of unnecessary costs. I would strongly advise you to make a will.'

A will is a legal document which says how your possessions (your *estate*) are to be dealt with when you die. Even if your estate is small and your intentions regarding it extremely simple, you should still make a will. If you do not, a number of problems can arise, as follows:

- your survivors may waste time trying to find out whether or not you did write a will; it may take them a long time to trace all your possessions; and they may have to spend time and money tracing relatives
- if there is no will, it may take longer and cost more to 'prove' the estate (an administrative process which has to be completed before your estate can be 'distributed' – that is, handed on – to your heirs)

- without a will, your next of kin (often a wife or husband) will usually be appointed to sort out your affairs. At the time of bereavement, he/she may prefer not to take on this role and you may, in any case, have friends or relatives who would be more suited to the task
- the law will dictate how your estate is passed on and this may not coincide with your wishes
- the law may require that various trusts are set up with the trust assets invested in particular ways. The terms of these trusts may be overly restrictive and, especially where small sums are involved, unnecessarily large expenses may be incurred
- your heirs may have to pay inheritance tax (or more tax) than would have been the case had you used your will to pass on your possessions tax-efficiently (see Chapter 14).

Apart from avoiding these problems and ensuring that your possessions are given away as you would choose, a will can be used for other purposes too: you can appoint guardians to care for young children; and you can express your preferences about funeral arrangements and any wishes about the use of your body for medical purposes after death.

Note that the rules relating to wills and intestacy in Scotland differ in a number of respects from the rules for the rest of the UK – see page 164. The rules described here apply to England and Wales.

Definitions

Three types of player are involved in a will:

- *testator/testatrix* The man or woman whose will it is. You must be aged 18 or over (and of sound mind) to make a valid will
- *beneficiary* A person or organisation left something ('benefits') under a will
- *personal representative* The person, people or organisation that sees that your estate is distributed following your death. If you have not made a will, they are your *administrators* and they will distribute your estate in accordance with the law. If you have made a will, they are your *executors* and they will try to ensure that the instructions in your will are carried out.

Dying without a will

If you die without making a will ('intestate') the law dictates how your estate will be passed on (with the exception of joint assets held under a 'joint tenancy' – see page 115 – which pass automatically to the surviving co-owners). The law aims, in the first instance, to protect your immediate family – husband or wife, and children. This might coincide with your wishes but, even if it did, it still might not result in your estate being used as you had expected or would have wished. Furthermore, people who are not formally part of your family – for example, an unmarried partner – have no automatic rights under the intestacy laws (though they might still have a claim against your estate – see page 162).

Where part or all of your estate would pass to your spouse under the intestacy rules, this will only happen if he or she survives you by at least 28 days. This 'survivorship provision' (which is a common device used in wills) makes sure that, in cases where you and your spouse die within a short time of one another (for example, as a result of a road traffic accident), the relatives of each of you benefit from your respective estates rather than everything going to the relatives of the second to die.

The intestacy laws assume that all your possessions could be sold by your personal representative to convert your whole estate into cash which would then be distributed according to the rules described below. In practice, the possessions would not necessarily be sold and could be passed on intact, but problems can arise where there is a large possession – for example, the family home – if it needs to be split between two or more beneficiaries. The intestacy laws operate as follows.

If you are survived by a husband or wife and no children

Your husband or wife is entitled to all your *personal chattels* (i.e. personal possessions, such as clothes, furniture, jewellery, private cars and so on). If your estate is valued at £200,000 or less, your husband or wife also inherits the whole estate. (See Chapter 13 for guidance on valuing your estate.)

If your estate is valued at more than £200,000, your husband or wife gets the whole lot, provided you had no living parents or brothers or sisters at the time of your death. If you are survived by parents, brothers or sisters, your husband or wife is entitled to a fixed sum of £200,000 (plus interest at a set rate from the date of death until the date the payment is made) plus half of whatever remains. The remainder goes to your parents or, if they are dead, to your brothers and sisters. Chart 12.1 summarises the position.

Chart 12.1 Who inherits if you leave a husband/wife and no children

Is your estate worth more than £200,000?	→	NO →	Husband/wife inherits whole estate
↓			
YES			
↓			
Do you have parents?	→	YES →	Husband/wife gets £200,000 (with interest)
↓			plus half the remaining
NO			estate. Your parents
			inherit the rest.
↓			
Do you have brothers or sisters?	→	YES →	Husband/wife gets £200,000 (with interest)
↓			plus half the remaining
NO			estate. Your brothers
			and sisters (or their
↓			children) share the rest.
Husband/wife inherits whole estate			

EXAMPLE 12.1

Jeremy and Ali had been married for ten years when tragically Jeremy died in a road accident. He was only 36 and, though he had several times thought about making a will, he had not got around to doing it. His estate was valued at £250,000 and he would have left everything to Ali, but under the intestacy laws the estate was divided between Ali and his parents as follows:

Ali's share

Fixed sum	£200,000
plus interest	£4,940
plus half the remaining estate	
(i.e. £250,000 – £204,940) ÷ 2	£22,530
Total	£227,470
Jeremy's parents' share	£22,530

If you are survived by children

If you leave children, but no husband or wife, the inheritance position is simple: your children share your estate equally. Note that 'children' includes offspring from your most recent marriage (if applicable), any previous marriages, adopted children and illegitimate children. However, it does not include stepchildren.

If you are survived by a husband or wife, he or she is entitled to all your personal possessions. And, if your estate is valued at £125,000 or less, he or she also inherits the whole of that.

If your estate is valued at more than £125,000, your husband or wife receives a fixed sum of £125,000 (plus interest at a set rate from the date of death until the date payment is made) and a life interest in half of the remaining estate. A life interest gives him or her the right to the income from that part of the estate (or use of it in the case of, say, a house), but he or she cannot touch the capital. (Note that the husband or wife can decide to take an appropriately calculated lump sum from the estate in place of a life interest.) The rest of the estate passes to your children to be shared equally between them. They also become entitled to the capital bearing the life interest when your husband or wife dies. (Note that children can inherit capital outright only once they reach the age of 18, so they have an income entitlement up to that age.) Chart 12.2 summarises the position.

Chart 12.2   Who inherits if you leave children

| Do you have a husband or wife? | → | NO | → | Your children inherit equal shares in the estate |

↓

YES

↓

| Is your estate worth more than £125,000? | → | NO | → | Husband/wife inherits whole estate |

↓

YES

↓

Husband/wife gets £125,000 (with interest) plus life interest in half the remaining estate (which passes eventually to your children). Your children inherit the rest.

EXAMPLE 12.2

Alan died leaving an estate valued at £250,000. Of this amount £200,000 represented his half-share in the family home (which he and his wife, Julia, owned as tenants in common – see page 115). However, he had made no will. Under the intestacy rules Julia and his only child inherited the estate in the following shares:

Julia's share

Capital: fixed sum	£125,000
plus interest	£3,090
Total capital	£128,090
Remaining estate (£250,000 – £128,090)	£121,910

So Julia also gets income/use from half of £121,910 i.e. £60,955

Child's share

Capital now	£60,955
Capital to be set aside for future	£60,955

Unfortunately, Julia's outright inheritance of £128,090 and interest in a further £60,955 come to less than the value of the family home. In order to comply with the intestacy rules requiring capital of £121,910 in total to be set aside for the child, part of the family home must be held in trust for the child.

If you are survived by no near relatives

If you leave no husband or wife and no children, the intestacy rules rank your heirs in the order in which they will inherit your estate.

Chart 12.3 Who inherits if you leave no near relatives

Are you survived by your parents?	→	YES	→	Your parents inherit equal shares in your estate
↓				
NO				
↓				
Do you have any brothers or sisters?	→	YES	→	Your brothers and sisters inherit equal shares in your estate[†]
↓				
NO				
↓				
Are you survived by any grandparents?	→	YES	→	Your grandparents inherit the estate in equal shares
↓				
NO				
↓				
Do you have any uncles or aunts?	→	YES	→	Your uncles and aunts inherit the estate in equal shares[‡]
↓				
NO				
↓				
Your estate passes to the Crown				

[†]If a brother or sister has died before you, their offspring, if any, inherit instead. If you have no full brothers or sisters, any half-brothers or half-sisters will share the estate instead.
[‡]If any uncle or aunt has died before you, their offspring inherit instead. If you have no full uncles or aunts, any half-uncles or half-aunts share the estate instead.

If you have no relatives who are eligible to inherit (see Chart 12.3), your estate passes to the Crown in *bona vacantia* (which literally means 'unclaimed goods'). The Crown may make ex gratia payments if your dependants or relatives make an application to it. It is important to realise that claimants have no *right* to receive anything – payments are at the discretion of the Crown. Applicants who are most likely to succeed include the following:

- someone who had a long, close association with you: for example, an unmarried partner or someone who lived with you as a child
- someone whom you clearly intended to benefit under a will that was invalid for some reason.

EXAMPLE 12.3

Harold died aged 89. He was an only child. His wife and parents died before him and he himself had no children. But his Uncle Jack (who died long ago) had two children, Jean and Richard, who are both still living. They each inherit half of Harold's estate.

Partial intestacy

Your will should cover all your assets. If you do not specify how part of your estate is to be used, that part will be subject to the intestacy rules even though the rest of your estate is disposed of in accordance with the will.

Problems caused by intestacy

The main problems of intestacy arise where you are survived by a partner (either married or not) and/or you have children. Unless you make a will, you cannot be certain that they will be adequately provided for in the event of your death.

If you are not married to your partner, he or she has no automatic right of inheritance in the event of your death. However, he or she will be able to claim a share of your estate under the Inheritance (Provision for Family and Dependants) Act 1975 if they lived with you as husband or wife throughout the two years prior to your death. If that condition does not apply, they may still be able to claim support from your estate, if they can show that they were being partly or wholly maintained by you when you were alive. In either case, a claim must usually be made within six months of permission being granted to distribute the estate. It will then be considered by the courts, which is generally a lengthy and often costly procedure.

If you are married, there is a tendency to assume that your husband or wife will automatically inherit everything. The foregoing sections have shown that this is by no means certain. And, even if you are happy for your husband or wife and children to share your assets, the practical application of the intestacy rules may be very distressing to your survivors. Where the estate must be shared between husband or wife and children, or husband or wife and other relatives, your husband or wife has the right to claim the family home as part or all of his or her inheritance (provided he or she lived there with you prior to your death). If the home is worth more than the amount he or she is entitled to inherit, your husband or wife can 'buy' the excess from the estate. But if he or she does not have sufficient resources to be able to do this, the home may have to be sold so that the cash raised can be split as required by the intestacy provisions.

The intestacy laws are very rigid concerning the inheritance of assets by children. The assets must usually be converted to cash and placed in trust where they are to be invested in a restricted range of 'safe' assets. This can cause a number of problems: first, it may be more desirable to keep the assets rather than convert them to cash; secondly, the amount involved may really be so small that setting up a trust may be disproportionately expensive. The yield on the 'safe' investments might be lower than is required to keep pace with inflation and will generally be lower than the return available on many other investments – this can result in an inadequate income for a husband or wife who has a lifetime interest in the income from the assets.

Intestacy in Scotland

The law in Scotland works differently for those who die without making a will:

- **If you were married with no children** Your husband or wife has 'prior rights' to the family home (provided it is in Scotland) up to a value of £110,000, furniture and household effects up to £20,000 and a cash sum up to £50,000. He or she also has 'legal rights' to half the remaining 'moveable estate' (i.e. excluding land and buildings). See below for the remaining estate.

- **If you were married with children** Your husband or wife has prior rights to the family home up to £110,000, furniture and effects up to £20,000 and a cash sum up to £30,000 plus legal rights to share one-third of the remaining moveable estate between them. The children also have legal rights to share one-third of the moveable estate between them. See below for the remaining estate.

- **If you had children but no husband or wife** The children have legal rights to half the moveable estate.

- **The remaining estate** Whatever remains after prior and legal rights, or in a case where there is no husband, wife or child, passes to relatives in this order of priority: brothers and sisters (or their children) and/or parents, uncles and aunts (or their children), grandparents, great-uncles and aunts (or their children), great-grandparents and so on until some relative is found to inherit. If no surviving relatives can be traced, the estate passes to the Crown. (The division of estates within the above classes can be complex so, if you need further information, you should seek legal advice.)

Intestacy in Northern Ireland

The law is also different in Northern Ireland for those who die without making a will:

- **If you were married with no children** Your husband or wife inherits all your personal effects plus the first £200,000 of your estate and half of any residue. The remainder passes to parent(s) or brothers and sisters if there are no parents still living.

- **If you were married with children** Your husband or wife inherits all your personal effects plus the first £125,000 of your estate plus half of any residue if there is one child, or one-third of the residue, if there are more children. The remainder of the estate passes to the child(ren) – in trust if they are aged under 18.

- **If you had children but no husband or wife** The estate is divided equally between the children.
- **If you had no children and no husband or wife** Your estate goes to your relatives, starting wtih parents, but extending to very distant relatives if no closer ones survive you.

Drawing up a will

In many people's minds, making a will is inextricably linked with using a solicitor, but this need not be so. Provided your personal circumstances are not overly complicated and you understand what you are doing, there is no reason why you should not write your own will. A number of books and kits are available to help you do this: for example, Which? Books' *Wills and Probate* or *Make Your Own Will* Action Pack.[25] The main advantage of writing your own will is, of course, the saving in solicitor's fees. But a simple will, for example involving only personal (no business) assets in the UK, with everything left to your husband or wife, need not cost much. If your affairs are more complex, you should be wary of the DIY route.

A will, to fulfil its purpose, must record your intentions clearly and unambiguously and should include contingency plans to cover the possibility, for example, of a beneficiary dying before you. There are also various pitfalls to be avoided – some that would invalidate the will and leave your estate subject to the intestacy laws, and others which would not invalidate the will but would interfere with the intentions expressed in it. For example, a valid will must be signed by two or more witnesses, who may not also be beneficiaries under the will; so, if you are leaving anything to your husband or wife, say, do not ask him or her to be a witness – the will would be valid, but your spouse would not be allowed to inherit under it.

If your affairs are complicated – e.g. you run your own business, you have been divorced or you have step-children – or you do not feel confident about your knowledge of the law relating to wills, you

---

[25] Available from Which? Ltd, PO Box 44, Hertford X SG14 1SH or Freephone 0800 252100 or fax Freephone 0800 533053 to order on Mastercard/Visa.

would be wise to employ a professional rather than trying to draw up a will yourself. But how good are the professionals? *Which?* has tested a selection of different will-writing professionals and the results are shown in Table 12.1.

Table 12.1 Will-writers on test

Type of will-writer	Cost of a simple will	Number of wills tested	How the wills were rated		
			Good	Average	Poor
Solicitors	£30–£125	19	47%	26%	26%
Will-writing firms	£25–£75	25	12%	52%	36%
Banks, building societies and insurance companies	£40–£60	7	0%	86%	14%

Source: *Which?* October 1996

Solicitors are the traditional profession to turn to for a will. Generally, you meet face-to-face with the solicitor who will draft your will either at the firm's offices or possibly at your home. Solicitors go through a rigorous training procedure before they qualify and carry on training while they practise through a system of continuous professional development. In the *Which?* test they produced the highest proportion of 'good' wills, but even so a quarter of wills produced by them were rated 'poor' by the *Which?* panel of experts. Problems encountered included a will which did not express the client's intentions, failure to consider trusts and guardians for young children and a long delay in producing a draft will. All solicitors in England and Wales are covered by a complaints procedure run by the Office for the Supervision of Solicitors★ (which replaced the Solicitors Complaints Bureau). In Scotland and Northern Ireland, you can take any complaints to the respective Law Society.★

There are also a growing number of will-writing services. These are often small firms working under a franchise or as agents of a larger company. Most work by gathering the necessary details from you and feeding these into a computer which produces your will. Unlike solicitors, people running, or working for, will-writing firms are not required to have any formal legal qualifications, though they will probably have received some initial training and the computer software they are using will have been developed using legal experts; these firms may use a solicitor to draw up complicated wills. In the past, problems have arisen with some of these services: a number of firms have gone bust and, in one case, it was found that a potentially large number of the wills written contained a flaw and might not be valid. The will-writing firms came out worst in the *Which?* survey with over a third of the wills rated as poor. *Which?* found no difference between large and small firms; both tended to use standardised formats and often failed to get the details right. No independent complaints mechanism exists for will-writing firms. Three trade bodies – the Society of Will Writers,★ the Willwriter's Association★ and the Institute of Professional Willwriters★ – aim to regulate their members, but membership is not compulsory and it's not clear whether their regulation is effective.

The third group tested by *Which?* was banks, building societies and life insurance companies. They offer will preparation but a few insist that you agree to them also acting as executors of the will (which is not generally a good idea – see below). You have an interview with the bank, society or company either at their offices or in your home. The interviewer you meet is not usually the person who actually draws up the will. In general, the survey found these wills to be adequate but not going into the depth needed to cover every eventuality. If a bank or building society writes the will and you have a complaint, you can go to the Banking Ombudsman★ or Building Societies Ombudsman,★ respectively. No independent complaints body covers insurance companies drafting wills.

Overall, from the survey there seems to be no best choice for drawing up your will. Banks, building societies and insurance . companies are the most consistent but a good solicitor will be better. Recommendations from family and friends may be helpful.

Appointing executors

You have a choice when it comes to deciding who will sort out your affairs for you in accordance with your will: you can appoint a professional as your executor – e.g. a solicitor or your bank – or you can appoint friends or relatives. In general, professionals often charge more and if problems arise, such as long delays, the beneficiaries can do little because they do not themselves have a contract with the executor, so have little access to information and limited power to challenge the executor's actions. If, instead, you appoint relatives or friends, they always have the option to employ a solicitor direct if they need help.

You can choose anyone you like to act as executor – it's common to appoint the main beneficiary. Normally, you should appoint two executors, just in case one dies before you or refuses to act. Make sure you ask the people concerned whether they would be willing to take on the role.

Renewing your will

You should not view making a will as a task once done to be forgotten. As your circumstances alter, so your will needs to be updated. In some situations – for example, if you marry or remarry – any will made before the marriage will automatically be invalidated (unless it was a will made specifically in contemplation of the marriage). All bequests and references to your ex-husband or ex-wife are automatically revoked by divorce, and the appointment of your 'ex' as guardian of any children will be revoked, unless you have made clear that this is still your intention. In other respects, the rest of your will stands. The same is not true of separation – the whole will including bequests to your spouse is still valid; in that situation, you should review the terms of your will. Other circumstances in which you might want to revise your will are the birth or adoption of a child, or if you decide that you would like to leave a legacy to a charity. It is wise to read through your will every two years, say, as a matter of course, to check that it reflects your current wishes. If you do decide to alter a will – even slightly – it is better to draw up a new will containing the revisions than to add an amendment (a 'codicil'). The trouble with codicils is that they can easily become detached from the will and lost. A new will should always start with a clause revoking any previous wills; this automatically invalidates any earlier wills. (Interestingly, if a will is not automatically revoked – by, say, a later will or marriage – the law requires that you *physically* destroy your will if it is to be revoked. Simply putting a cross through it and scribbling 'cancelled' or 'revoked' across it would not be enough.)

Making gifts in your will

In your will, you can give away anything you own. There are different types of gift, and the distinction between them is important both for tax reasons (see Chapter 13) and because of the order in which they can be redirected to meet expenses and settle debts that you leave at the time of your death. The main types of gift are described as follows.

Specific gift

This can be a named or identifiable possession such as a piece of furniture, an item of jewellery or a particular car. It may be a specific possession that you own *at the time you write the will*; if you later sell the item the beneficiary who was to have received it will get nothing after all.

Alternatively, you might leave a more general type of specific gift. This would be the gift of a possession but not restricted to a specific item that you own at the time of drawing up the will. For example, you might give away 'the car I own at the time of my death', which would take into account the possibility that you might change your car from time to time.

A specific gift might be even more widely defined: for example, simply 'a car'. In this latter case, the executors of your will would have a duty to make sure that the beneficiary received a car – either one that you owned at the time of death or, if you had none, one bought specifically to fulfil the terms of the will – or, alternatively, the trustees would have to pay over an equivalent sum of money.

Legacies

A 'pecuniary legacy' is a particular type of specific gift which is a straightforward gift of money: for example, '£1,000 to my niece, Claire'.

A 'demonstrative legacy' can be either a general gift or a pecuniary legacy which is to be paid from a specific fund: for example, 'a violin to be paid for out of my account with Barclays Bank' or '£1,000 from my account with the Halifax Building Society'. If there was not enough money in the account, the shortfall would have to be met by using other assets in the estate.

Residuary gift

A will which assigned every part of your estate as a particular gift or legacy would be out of date almost immediately, because the value of your estate fluctuates even in the course of your daily transactions and will alter more widely during the course of time. Therefore, it is usual to leave whatever remains of your estate, after all your debts, expenses and various gifts as listed above have been paid, as a 'residuary gift' or 'residue'. You may intend your residue to be a substantial gift, or it may be a small amount with, say, the bulk of your estate given away through pecuniary gifts.

To meet debts and expenses, any intestate part of your estate will be used up first, followed by the residue.

EXAMPLE 12.4

Daisy died at the ripe old age of 92. Her sole survivor, Albert, had expected to inherit a sizeable sum. However, Daisy had already given Hadley Hall to Albert and clearly considered that was enough, because out of the £750,000 estate that she left, she gave £600,000 to a spread of charities. After deducting outstanding debts, funeral expenses and a very small tax bill, Albert inherited the residue of only £20,000.

Gifts you do not want to make

By omission, your will can also express your intention not to leave anything (or only very little) to people who might have expected to inherit from you. However, if these people were dependent on you (or you had a partner who had lived with you for at least two years as husband or wife without necessarily being dependent), they have the right to make a claim through the courts under the Inheritance (Provision for Family and Dependants) Act 1975 for reasonable provision out of your estate. The main people who are entitled to make such a claim are as follows:

- your husband or wife
- a former husband or wife, provided he or she has not remarried (and is not precluded from making a claim under the divorce settlement)

- a child of yours (whether legitimate, illegitimate or adopted)
- a child of your family (i.e. a stepchild or foster child)
- an unmarried partner.

An application under the Act must usually be made within six months of the personal representatives being given permission to dispose of the estate, though the court can extend this time limit. The court decides whether or not the applicant is entitled to financial support from the estate and, if it decides in favour of the applicant, it can order the payment of either a lump sum or income (or both).

You might seek to anticipate and thwart such a claim by giving away as much of your estate as possible, but this strategy will not work, because the court has the power to revoke such gifts in order to ensure that enough funds are available to meet the needs of your surviving dependants.

You can include in your will a statement setting out your reasons for excluding your dependants and the court will take this into account. It would be worth seeking advice from a solicitor about the most effective wording to use.

In Scotland, you cannot disinherit your husband, wife or children, who can claim their 'legal rights' to part of your estate. For more information see *Wills and Probate* published by Which? Limited.

Chapter 13

Tax at the time of death

NOT JUST A RICH MAN'S TAX

'When I die, my will is very simple,' said Percy, draining his glass. 'I haven't so very much to leave behind, but I'll give my son a bit to help him with his business. Then, I'll just split what's left between the wife and Rose.'

'You should watch out,' replied his friend as he rose to buy another round. 'If there is any tax to pay, it will probably come out of Rose's share – she might end up with a lot less than you're hoping.'

When you die, you are deemed to make a gift of all your possessions just before death. There is no capital gains tax (CGT) on your estate, but there might be inheritance tax (IHT) on the estate and there could be extra tax due on gifts which you had made in the seven years before death.

Tax on gifts made before death

Chapter 8 looked at the immediate tax position of gifts made during your lifetime. In the case of potentially exempt transfers (PETs) there was no tax to pay at the time of the gift, but if you die within seven years of making a PET, the gift becomes a 'chargeable transfer' and tax is due. The effective rate of tax ranges from 8 per cent up to 40 per cent, depending on the time that has elapsed since you originally made the gift (see page 105).

Similarly, a chargeable transfer – on which tax may have been paid at the time of the gift but at the lower lifetime IHT rate of 20 per cent – will be reassessed and there may be further tax to pay if you die within seven years of making the gift (see page 103).

The reassessment of these earlier gifts and the payment of any tax which becomes due on them is entirely separate from the calculation of tax on your estate. However, if you made PETs within seven years of dying, the fact that they have been reassessed as chargeable gifts will increase your running total up to the time of death, and that could create an IHT bill, or increase the amount of IHT payable, on your estate. What's more, there is no 'taper relief' (see page 105) on any extra tax payable on the estate due to the reassessment of PETs. This is a constant source of confusion, but taper relief can apply only to tax on the reassessed PETs themselves; taper relief has no impact whatsoever on extra tax on the estate.

Tax on your estate

On your death, IHT is due on the value of your estate plus your running total of gifts made in the seven years before death if they come to more than the tax-free slice. The tax-free slice for 1999–2000 is £231,000. See Chapter 8 for previous years' figures. This may seem a large sum, but £231,000 can soon be swallowed up, especially if you own your own home. Your estate is made up of:

- the value of all your possessions at the time of death, including your home, car, personal belongings, cash, investments, and so on
- *plus* any gifts with reservation (see page 108) that you made
- *plus* the proceeds of any insurance policies which are paid to your estate
- *less* your debts
- *less* reasonable funeral expenses.

This total is called your 'free estate' and it is the amount that is available for giving away. For the purpose of calculating any IHT, you can deduct from the free estate any gifts made in your will that count as tax-free gifts (see below). But you must *add* all the PETs and other taxable gifts which you made in the seven years before death to find the relevant running total. If the running total comes to more than the tax-free slice, inheritance tax at a rate of 40 per cent is payable.

Gifts under your will

If the value of your estate plus taxable gifts in the seven years before death comes to less than the tax-free slice, making gifts under your will is fairly straightforward: assuming that the estate is sufficiently large (after paying off debts and expenses), the recipients will receive the amounts that you specify in your will.

However, if there is inheritance tax due on the estate, matters are not always so simple. To work out how much the recipients will actually receive, you need to know how tax will be allocated between the various gifts. For IHT purposes, there are three types of gift which you can leave in a will:

- *tax-free gifts* (see above and Chapter 6)   There is no tax at all on these
- *free-of-tax gifts* (not to be confused with tax-free gifts)   The recipient gets the amount you specify and any tax due is paid out of the residue of the estate
- *gifts which bear their own tax*   With these, the amount you give is treated as a gross gift *out of which* the recipient must pay any tax due.

In general, a specific gift under your will is automatically treated as a free-of-tax gift unless it is tax-free or you have explicitly stated that the gift should bear its own tax. But, to avoid confusion, it is a good idea to state for every gift whether it is 'free-of-tax' or 'to bear its own tax'.

Whatever is left of your estate after deducting specific gifts is called the 'residue' or 'residuary gift'. The residue can be either a tax-free gift or taxable, in which case it bears its own tax. The residue may be split, with part counting as a tax-free gift and part as a taxable one.

The fun starts when you try to calculate how much tax will be deducted either from the residue of the estate or from the specific gifts. The calculations vary depending on the mix of gifts which you are making. The following sections describe the main possibilities.

If you find the calculations that follow daunting, do not despair – you can ask your solicitor or accountant to work out for you the tax position of various gifts that you are considering as part of your will. The most important point is that you should be aware that tax can affect the gifts in different ways.

If all your gifts are tax-free

This is the simplest case. As with lifetime gifts, some gifts from your estate are free of IHT, in particular: gifts of any amount to your husband or wife, gifts to charities, gifts for the public benefit, gifts to political parties and gifts to Housing Associations (see Chapter 6 for more details).

So, for example, you might make a gift to charity and leave the residue to your husband or wife. Since both types of gift are tax-free, there is no inheritance tax at all.

EXAMPLE 13.1

When Connie dies in October 1999, she leaves an estate made up as follows:

Cottage	£65,000
Personal possessions	£21,500
Cash in bank	£496
Investments	£331,204
Gross value of estate	£418,200
less various small debts	£500
less funeral expenses, administration costs, etc.	£2,700
Net value of 'free estate'	£415,000

Connie had made no gifts during the previous seven years. Since the value of the estate exceeds the tax-free slice, you might expect IHT to have been payable, but in fact it was not because Connie used the whole of the 'free estate' to make tax-free gifts. She left a legacy of £100,000 to charity and the residue to her husband.

If all your specific gifts bear their own tax

Again, this is a relatively simple case. The amount of tax on each gift is in proportion to the values of chargeable gifts. This is done by working out the tax due on the whole of the chargeable estate and then expressing this as a percentage of the chargeable estate – this gives you an 'effective' IHT rate. The effective rate is then applied to each gift that is to bear its own tax to find out the amount of tax due on the gift. Example 13.2 should make this clear.

EXAMPLE 13.2

Jim dies in July 1999 leaving an estate of £500,000. He makes two specific gifts bearing their own tax: £100,000 to his friend Ben and £180,000 to his cousin Gerald. He leaves the residue to his wife. Jim made no PETs or chargeable transfers in the seven years before he died. The tax position is worked out as follows:

TAX POSITION OF THE ESTATE

Value of free estate	£500,000
less tax-free gifts (i.e. residue to his wife)	£220,000
Chargeable part of estate	£280,000
less tax-free slice	£231,000
	£49,000
Tax on £49,000 @ 40%	£19,600
Effective tax rate ([£19,600 ÷ £280,000] x 100)	7%

WHO GETS WHAT

Tax on Ben's gift @ 7%	£7,000
Net amount Ben receives	£93,000
Tax on Gerald's gift @ 7%	£12,600
Net amount Gerald receives	£167,400
Amount left to wife	£220,000

If all your specific gifts are free of tax

The main complication in this situation is that, when the estate pays the tax due (out of the residue), it is deemed to be making a gift of the tax as well. To take account of this, all the free-of-tax gifts must be 'grossed up', which simply means that you find the total that equals the amount of the actual gifts plus the tax on them. The tax is then deducted from the residue.

EXAMPLE 13.3

Alec also dies in July 1999 leaving an estate of £500,000. He makes two specific gifts which are free of tax: £100,000 to his friend Douglas and £180,000 to his friend Annette. He leaves the residue to his wife. Alec made no PETs or chargeable transfers in the seven years before he died. The tax position is worked out as follows:

GROSSING UP THE GIFTS

[1]*Add together* all free-of-tax gifts (£100,000 + £180,000)	£280,000
[2]*less* tax-free slice	£231,000
	£49,000
[3]gross up (see page 213) at the 40% tax rate (i.e. divide by 1 — 40% = 0.6)	£81,667
The grossed-up value of the gifts is £81,667 + £231,000	£312,667

TAX POSITION OF THE ESTATE

[4]Value of estate	£500,000
less tax-free part of the estate (£500,000 – £312,667)	£187,333
[5]Chargeable estate	£312,667

less tax-free slice	£231,000
	£81,667
[6]Tax on £81,667 @ 40%	£32,667

WHO GETS WHAT

Net amount Douglas receives	£100,000
Net amount Annette receives	£180,000
Amount left to wife	
[7](£500,000 − £100,000 − £180,000 − £32,667)	£187,333

Notes

1 The free-of-tax gifts are added together. This is not their taxable value, because they need first to be grossed up. Note that, at this stage, we do not know what part of the estate is tax-free, because we do not know yet how much tax must be deducted before the residue passes to Alec's wife.

2 We do not gross up the whole of the free-of-tax gifts, because some falls within the tax-free slice. Therefore, at this step, we deduct the tax-free slice to leave just the (net) value of the gifts which are to be taxed.

3 The gifts are grossed up at the death rate and the tax-free slice is added back to give the full grossed-up value of the free-of-tax gifts.

4 We now have the information to find the tax-free part of the estate. (The arithmetic seems circular in this example, but using this method allows us to deal with more complicated examples later on.)

5 The value of the estate less the tax-free part leaves the chargeable estate.

6 Tax is due on the chargeable estate less the tax-free slice at the death rate of 40 per cent.

7 There is, of course, no tax deducted from the free-of-tax gifts. All the tax is paid out of the residue, so the amount left to Alec's wife is the value of his estate less the gifts to other people less the tax bill.

If you leave a mixture of free-of-tax gifts and other types of taxable gift

This is the most complex situation. Problems arise because the free-of-tax gifts must be grossed up by the IHT rate, but initially the appropriate rate is not known because it is worked out in relation to the *whole* chargeable estate (which includes the gifts bearing their own tax as well). The problem is solved by splitting the calculation into two stages.

First, the free-of-tax gifts are grossed up by the full death rate of 40 per cent. The rest of the chargeable estate is added and IHT worked out in the normal way – but the result is only a notional amount of IHT. If notional IHT is divided by the size of the chargeable estate, this gives an assumed notional rate of IHT.

Now the second stage of the calculation can proceed. The notional rate of IHT is used to re-gross up the free-of-tax gifts. As before, the rest of the chargeable estate is added and tax is worked out in the normal way (using the 40 per cent death rate). Dividing the tax bill by the total chargeable estate gives the 'final estate rate' which is used to apportion the tax between the different chargeable gifts. See Example 13.4.

You will need to do the same sort of calculation if, in addition to leaving free-of-tax gifts, you also divide the residue so that part is tax-free and part is taxable – this would be the position, for example, if you divided the residue between your children and your husband or wife. The taxable part of the residue is treated as if it is a gross gift bearing its own tax, so it does not need to be grossed up. See Example 13.5.

EXAMPLE 13.4

Suppose, in Example 13.3, Alec left £100,000 free of tax to Douglas and £180,000 free of tax to Annette, as before, but also left a gift of £10,000 to bear its own tax to his daughter Judy. He leaves the residue to his wife. The tax position is as follows:

STAGE 1
GROSSING UP THE GIFTS

[1]*Add together* all free-of-tax gifts (£100,000 + £180,000)	£280,000
[2]*less* tax-free slice	£231,000
	£49,000
[3]gross up at the 40% tax rate (i.e. divide by 0.6)	£81,667
The grossed-up value of the gifts is £81,667 + £231,000	£312,667

TAX POSITION OF THE ESTATE

[4]Value of estate	£500,000
less tax-free part of estate	
(£500,000 – £312,667 – £10,000)	£177,333
[5]Chargeable estate	£322,667
less tax-free slice	£231,000
	£91,667
[6]Tax on £91,667 @ 40%	£36,667
[7]Notional rate of IHT ([£36,667 ÷ £322,667] x 100)	11.364%

STAGE 2

[8]RE-GROSSING UP THE GIFTS

Total free-of-tax gifts	£280,000
gross up at the notional IHT rate	
(i.e. divide by 1—0.11364 = 0.886)	
Re-grossed-up value of free-of-tax gift	£315,898

REVISED TAX POSITION OF THE ESTATE

[9]Value of estate	£500,000
less tax-free part of estate	
(£500,000 – £315,898 – £10,000)	£174,102
New total for chargeable estate	£325,898
less tax-free slice	£231,000
	£94,898
[10]Tax @ 40% on £94,898	£37,959
Final estate rate ([£37,959 ÷ £325,898] x 100)	11.648%

WHO GETS WHAT

[11]Tax on Judy's gift @ 11.648%	£1,165
Net amount Judy receives	£8,835
[12]Net amount Douglas receives	£100,000
Net amount Annette receives	£180,000
[13]Tax to be deducted from residue (£37,959 – £1,165)	£36,794
[14]Amount left to wife (£500,000 – £100,000 – £180,000 – £10,000 – £36,794)	£173,206

Notes

1 The free-of-tax gifts are added together. This is not their taxable value, because they need to be grossed up.

2 We do not gross up the whole of the free-of-tax gifts, because some fall within the tax-free slice. Therefore, at this step, we deduct the tax-free slice to leave just the (net) value of the gifts which are to be taxed. This is a simplification, because there is another taxable gift which should benefit from the tax-free slice.

3 The free-of-tax gifts are grossed up at the death rate (40%) and the tax-free slice is added back to give the full grossed-up value of the free-of-tax gifts. This is a first approximation, because we have yet to take account of the other taxable gift which will derive some benefit from the tax-free slice.

4 We now have the information to make a first approximation of the tax-free part of the estate. This is the value of the estate less the grossed-up free-of-tax gifts less the gift bearing its own tax.

5 The value of the estate less the tax-free part leaves our estimate of the chargeable estate.

6 Tax is worked out on this first approximation of the chargeable estate at the death rate of 40 per cent after deducting the tax-free slice.

7 Dividing the amount of tax by the value of the chargeable estate gives us the rate of IHT on the chargeable estate, called the 'notional rate'.

8 We can now get a more accurate figure for the gross value of the free-of-tax gifts by grossing them up at the notional rate of IHT.

9 The estate can now more accurately be divided into its elements: the tax-free part and the chargeable part.

10 Tax at the death rate can now be calculated on the chargeable part. This gives the actual tax bill to be divided between the various bequests. The rate of tax to be applied to each gift is found by dividing the tax bill by the value of the chargeable estate.

11 Judy's gift bears its own tax, so the amount she receives is reduced by the tax due.

12 The free-of-tax gifts are intact with tax on them being borne by the residue.

13 Tax to be deducted from the residue is the total tax bill less any tax being borne by particular bequests.

14 The residue is the value of the estate less the value of the bequests less the tax on the free-of-tax gifts. There is, of course, no tax deducted from the free-of-tax gifts. All the tax is paid out of the residue, so the amount left to the wife is the value of the estate less the gifts to other people less the tax bill.

EXAMPLE 13.5

Percy dies in October 1999 leaving an estate of £750,000. He makes a specific free-of-tax gift of £250,000 to his son, Harold, and leaves the residue equally to his wife and his daughter, Rose. Percy made no PETs or chargeable transfers in the seven years before he died. The tax position is worked out as follows:

STAGE 1
GROSSING UP THE GIFTS

[1]*Add together* all free-of-tax gifts	£250,000
[2]*less* tax-free slice	£231,000
	£19,000
[3]gross up at 40% tax rate (i.e. divide by 1 — 40% = 0.6)	£31,667
The grossed-up value of the gift is £31,667 + £231,000	£262,667

TAX POSITION OF THE ESTATE

[4]Value of estate	£750,000
less tax-free part of the estate (£750,000 – £262,667 – [residue ÷ 2])	£243,667
[5]Chargeable estate	£506,333
less tax-free slice	£231,000
	£275,333
[6]Tax on £275,333 @ 40%	£110,133
[7]Notional rate of IHT ([£110,333 ÷ £506,333] x 100)	21.751%

STAGE 2
[8]RE-GROSSING UP THE GIFTS

Free-of-tax gift	£250,000
gross up at the notional IHT rate (i.e. divide by [1−0.21751] = 0.78249)	
Re-grossed-up value of free-of-tax gift	£319,494

REVISED TAX POSITION OF THE ESTATE

[9]Value of estate	£750,000
less tax-free part of estate (£750,000 − £319,494 −([residue ÷ 2])	£215,253
New total for chargeable estate	£534,747
less tax-free slice	£231,000
	£303,747
[10]Tax @ 40% on £303,747	£121,499
Final estate rate ([£121,499 ÷ £534,747] x 100)	22.721%

WHO GETS WHAT

[11]Harold receives	£250,000
Tax on Harold's legacy @ 22.721% of £319,494 (to be borne by estate)	£72,592
[12]Residue (£750,000 − £250,000 − £72,592)	£427,408
[13]Wife receives (1/2 x £427,408)	£213,704
[14]Tax on Rose's share of the residue @ 22.721% x £213,704	£48,556
Rose receives (£213,704 − £48,556)	£165,148

Notes

1   The free-of-tax gifts are added together. This is not their taxable value, because they need to be grossed up.

2   We do not gross up the whole of the free-of-tax gifts, because some fall within the tax-free slice. Therefore, at this step, we deduct the tax-free slice to leave just the (net) value of the gifts which are to be taxed. This is a simplification, because another taxable gift (in this case, part of the residue) should benefit from the tax-free slice.

3   The free-of-tax gifts are grossed up at the death rate and the tax-free slice is added back to give the full grossed-up value of the free-of-tax gifts. This is a first approximation, because we have yet to take account of the other taxable gift which will derive some benefit from the tax-free slice.

4   We now have the information to make a first approximation of the tax-free part of the estate. This is the value of the estate less the grossed-up free-of-tax gift (£262,667) less half of what remains ([£750,000 − £262,667] ÷ 2), which will be a gift bearing its own tax.

5   The value of the estate less the tax-free part leaves our estimate of the chargeable estate.

6   Tax is worked out on this first approximation of the chargeable estate at the death rate of 40 per cent after deducting the tax-free slice.

7   Dividing the amount of tax by the value of the chargeable estate gives us the rate of IHT on the chargeable estate, called the 'notional rate'.

8   We can now get a more accurate figure for the gross value of the free-of-tax gifts by grossing them up at the notional rate of IHT.

9   The estate can now more accurately be divided into its elements: the tax-free part and the chargeable part. This latter comprises the re-grossed up gifts (£319,494) *plus* the taxable part of the residue ([£750,000 − £319,494] ÷ 2)

10 Tax at the death rate can now be calculated on the chargeable part. This gives the actual tax bill to be divided between the various bequests. The rate of tax to be applied to each gift is found by dividing the tax bill by the value of the chargeable estate.

11 The free-of-tax gift to Harold is intact with tax on it being borne by the residue.

12 The residue is the value of the estate less the value of the free-of-tax bequest less the tax on the free-of-tax gift (calculated at the final estate rate).

13 The wife receives half the residue as specified in the will.

14 The remaining half of the residue goes to Rose, but this is a taxable bequest. Tax is found by multiplying her half of the residue by the final estate rate. This substantially reduces Rose's share of the residue.

Quick-succession relief

If you left a substantial gift in your will to someone – for example, a son or daughter – who then died shortly after you, there could be two IHT bills on the same assets in a short space of time. To guard against this, a claim can be made for 'quick-succession relief'. This is available where the person inheriting the assets dies within five years of him or her becoming part of that person's estate (even if they are then sold or given away before the recipient's death). The relief is tapered: full relief is given if the recipient's death occurs within one year of the gift; a reduced rate applies if a longer time elapses (see Table 13.1).

Quick-succession relief is also available where the original gift was a lifetime gift and the recipient dies within five years. However, the amount of tax due, if any, on the original gift will not be known until seven years have passed since the gift was made, so there will be a delay before the amount of any relief can be calculated.

Table 13.1 Quick-succession relief

Years between first and second death	Tax relief on second death as a percentage of tax applicable to the original gift[†]
Up to 1	100
More than 1 and up to 2	80
More than 2 and up to 3	60
More than 3 and up to 4	40
More than 4 and up to 5	20
More than 5	no tax relief

[†]The percentage is multiplied by the formula:

$$\frac{G - T}{G} \times T$$

where G = the gross amount of the original gift
T = the tax paid on the original gift.

Passing on your business

Handing on your business is a complex matter. There are many different ways of arranging the transfer and which is appropriate for you will depend very much on your particular circumstances. You would be unwise to make plans without seeking professional advice from your accountant and a solicitor. Business planning is outside the scope of this book, but it is worth pointing out here the important reliefs against IHT that may be available to you and your heirs.

Business property relief

If, on death, your business passes to someone else, your personal representatives may be able to claim 'business property relief' which will reduce the value of the transfer of the business for IHT purposes and thus reduce or eliminate any IHT otherwise payable. To be eligible, you must have been in business for at least two years. Only 'qualifying' business assets attract relief; these are assets which are either:

- used wholly or mainly for the purpose of your business, *or*
- are required for future use by the business.

Assuming you operate your business as a sole trader or as a partner in a partnership, business property relief will be given at the higher rate of 100 per cent (from 9 March 1992 onwards) – that is, it could completely eliminate an IHT charge.

EXAMPLE 13.6

Gerald dies leaving a grocery business valued at £500,000 which he has run for the last ten years. In his will, he hands the business to his son, Paul. He also leaves £250,000 to his wife. The IHT position is as follows:

Value of free estate	£750,000
less tax-free gift to wife	£250,000
Value of grocery business	£500,000
less 100% business property relief	£500,000
Chargeable part of the estate	£0

Relief of 100 per cent is also available if you pass on a holding of shares of more than 25 per cent of the shares of an unquoted company (which includes companies traded on the Alternative Investment Market, or AIM). From 1996–7 onwards, 100 per cent relief was extended to holdings of 25 per cent or less in unquoted companies.

A lower rate of business property relief – set at 50 per cent since 9 March 1992 – is available to set against transfers of a *controlling* holding in a fully quoted company.

The rates of relief were increased in the 1992 Budget and are intended to take most handovers of family companies outside the IHT net. However, even 100 per cent relief will not necessarily entirely mitigate an IHT bill. In particular, you should note that if the business property is subject to a binding contract for sale, relief will not be given. This might be the case where, say, a partnership has arranged that the surviving partners will buy out the share of a partner who dies; the deceased partner's share of the business would not qualify for relief in this situation.

Most types of business can qualify for business property relief. The only exception is businesses whose sole or main activity is dealing in stocks, shares, land or various other investments.

Any IHT due after business property relief has been given can be paid by interest-free instalments over a period of ten years.

Agricultural property relief

Agricultural property relief – which is similar to business property relief – is available when a farm is handed on. The relief, which is given automatically and does not have to be claimed, is given against the agricultural value of the land and buildings. The equipment, stock and so on do not qualify for agricultural property relief, but they may qualify for business property relief (see page 186). Note that the agricultural value of the farm may be lower than the market value if, say, the land has development value – the excess will not qualify for agricultural property relief, though it may be eligible for business property relief.

To qualify for agricultural property relief, you must either have occupied the farm, or a share of it, for the purpose of farming for at least two years, or you must have owned the farm, or a share in it, for at least seven years. If you farmed the land yourself, relief is given at the higher rate of 100 per cent from 9 March 1992 onwards. If you let the land to someone else to farm, relief is restricted to the lower rate of 50 per cent.

As with business property relief, agricultural property relief is also not available if the farm is subject to a binding contract for sale (see page 187).

Any IHT due after relief has been given can be paid by interest-free instalments over a period of ten years.

Paying the tax

Your personal representative(s) are responsible for paying the IHT due on your estate (and any other taxes which are outstanding at your death). IHT is due six months after the end of the month in which death occurs. However, if your personal representatives finish preparing the accounts of your estate earlier than this, the IHT becomes payable immediately the accounts are submitted. Your representatives may be able to pay the IHT in ten equal yearly instalments.

Chapter 14
Inheritance planning

IT'S NEVER TOO LATE, BUT ...

'So you mean that we can, in effect, rewrite Dad's will to swap the gifts around and cut the tax bill?'

'Precisely, Miss Cale. The law does currently allow this,' said the solicitor, somewhat ponderously. 'However, I should point out that matters would have been a great deal simpler had Mr Cale made satisfactory arrangements *before* his death. There would have been considerably greater scope for minimising – or even eliminating – the inheritance tax bill had he done so.'

This chapter draws together a number of points discussed in earlier chapters and introduces some new ones to show what you can do to plan your giving through inheritance more precisely and tax-efficiently.

The particular strategies you adopt will depend largely on your personal intentions and circumstances. Although many of the points given below can be applied simply and with a minimum of paperwork, others are not so straightforward and may hide potential pitfalls that you should take into account. Always seek advice from, for example, a solicitor or accountant if you are in any doubt about a proposed course of action. And, if you are giving away large sums, get advice first.

There are two main aims to planning inheritance:

- to make sure that your estate is divided as you had wished
- to minimise the amount of tax to be paid on the estate.

Clearly, the two aims are interlinked since a lower inheritance tax (IHT) bill means that more of your estate is left to give to your family and friends. Strategies to meet either or both aims are discussed below.

Gifts when you die

Use your tax-free slice

Try to make use of your tax-free slice (which covers the first £231,000 of chargeable transfers in the 1999–2000 tax year), and bear in mind that some gifts – for example, to your husband or wife or to charity – are always tax-free.

It may be tempting simply to leave everything to your husband or wife, but this can mean an unnecessarily large tax bill when he or she dies (see Example 14.1).

EXAMPLE 14.1

Sam dies and leaves his whole estate of £200,000 to his wife, Harriet. Since this is a tax-free gift, there is no IHT to pay. When Harriet dies her free estate is valued at £300,000 and is left completely to their only child, Phyllis. There is IHT to pay on the estate calculated as follows:

Value of free estate	£300,000
less tax-free slice	£231,000
	£69,000
Tax on £69,000 @ 40%	£27,600

However, suppose instead that Sam had left £100,000 to Phyllis (on which no IHT would be payable because it would be covered by the tax-free slice) and the remaining £100,000 to Harriet. On Harriet's death, her estate would have been valued at £200,000. Giving this to Phyllis would have been completely covered by Harriet's tax-free slice, so no IHT would be payable. Straightforward planning to make use of Sam's tax-free slice would save £27,600 in tax.

If you and your husband or wife intend to leave something to your children, it may be best to draw up your wills so that whoever dies first leaves part of the estate directly to the children. This will ensure that at least some use is made of the available tax-free slice. The remainder of the estate can be left to the surviving spouse. If you can, arrange the wills so that both of you can make maximum use of your tax-free slices, but take care to ensure that the surviving spouse will have enough to meet financial needs.

Be aware of how gifts are taxed

Examples 13.2 and 13.3 in Chapter 13 are intentionally identical except that in one the gifts bear their own tax and in the other the gifts are free-of-tax. The outcomes highlight two important points which you should bear in mind when planning gifts under your will:

- a gift which bears its own tax will generally be smaller than a gift of the same size which is free of tax
- leaving free-of-tax gifts reduces the size of the residue. If you leave a lot of free-of-tax gifts, the residue may be reduced to a trivial amount (or nothing at all).

Using lifetime gifts

One way to reduce the IHT payable on your death is to reduce the size of your estate by making gifts during your lifetime. However, before going down this road, you must consider your own financial needs. Any IHT payable on your estate is not really your problem; it will simply reduce the amount by which others benefit from your estate. It is not worth jeopardising your financial security in order to reduce the IHT bill of your heirs. So the first planning point is: do not give away more than you can afford to do without.

Assuming that you can afford to make a number of gifts during your lifetime, you will obviously want to ensure that they do not themselves give rise to a large tax bill. Chapter 6 lists the gifts which you can make during your lifetime which are tax-free.

It is not enough to look only at the IHT position of lifetime gifts. You must also consider the capital gains tax (CGT) position (see Chapters 6, 7 and 11). Taking the two taxes together, the 'best' gifts to make will tend to be the following:

- cash gifts (always free of CGT) that qualify for an IHT exemption
- cash gifts that count as PETs (see page 104) for IHT purposes
- business assets that qualify for hold-over relief from CGT (see page 91) and count as PETs for IHT or qualify for business property relief
- other gifts that are exempt from IHT or that count as PETs and for which the CGT bill is relatively small due to unused CGT allowance, indexation allowance or CGT taper relief (see Chapter 7).

Make tax-free gifts

Particularly important for IHT purposes is your yearly tax-free exemption (see page 66), which lets you give away up to £3,000 each year without incurring any IHT liability. If you choose cash gifts, there will be no CGT either.

Another very useful gift which is free of IHT is normal expenditure out of income – this can be particularly handy when used in conjunction with an insurance policy (see pages 65 and 196).

For tax purposes alone, it is not generally worth making, in your lifetime, a gift which would in any case be tax-free on your death: for example, a gift to charity. A safer course would be to retain the assets in case you need to draw on them and make the desired gift in your will.

Give assets whose value will rise

If your aim is to reduce the value of your estate at the time you die, then it makes sense to give away assets whose value you expect to increase. In that way the increase will accrue to the recipient of the gift and will be outside your estate.

Gifts with reservation

It is very difficult to take advantage of the tax rules and at the same time retain the use or control of something you are giving away outright. If the recipient does not enjoy the full use of the gift and you will in some way benefit, the gift may be deemed a 'gift with reservation' under the IHT rules and it will still count as part of your estate until the reservation ends. For more details see pages 108 and 207.

Making use of trusts

One way in which you can retain control over something you give away is by putting it into trust (see Chapter 10).

Lifetime gifts to a trust

Generally, you cannot be a beneficiary or potential beneficiary of a trust you set up without the assets you put into it counting as a gift with reservation. However, your husband or wife can benefit under the trust without triggering these rules *provided* that you yourself in no way benefit from your spouse's interest in the trust. Even in the latter case, however, the income tax and CGT rules may make this type of arrangement unattractive (see page 123).

A further exception to the gift with reservation rules is that if you retain a reversionary interest (see page 137) in a trust to which you have given assets, the gift does not count as one with reservation.

If you have made a gift with reservation to a discretionary trust (see page 139) and the reservation ends (for example, you cease to be a potential beneficiary), you are deemed to have made a PET to the trust on the date the reservation ends. Since normally a gift to a discretionary trust counts as a chargeable gift, you can possibly use this anomaly to your advantage (see Example 14.2).

Beware of setting up more than one trust on the same day, if one of them is a discretionary trust. If you do, it may increase the periodic charge on the discretionary trust.

If you yourself inherit money or assets which are surplus to your needs, you might consider putting them into trust straight away to benefit your children or grandchildren – this is a practice known as 'generation skipping'. The transfer can often be made tax-efficiently through a 'deed of variation' or possibly a 'disclaimer' (see page 200).

EXAMPLE 14.2

In September 1996, Jarvis wanted to put £100,000 into a discretionary trust for the benefit of his adult children. But his running total of gifts over the last seven years already exceeded £150,000. If he had made the gift then, he would have incurred an immediate tax bill of 20% x £100,000 = £20,000. Instead, he made himself a potential beneficiary under the trust; the £100,000 counted as a gift with reservation, and thus it did not reduce the value of his estate and there was no immediate tax bill. In 1999, Jarvis alters the trust so that he can no longer benefit under it. This action 'triggers' his gift which then ceases to be part of his estate and counts as a PET. Provided Jarvis survives for seven years after 1999, there will be no IHT on the gift.

Wills and trusts

There are two situations in which setting up a trust in your will can be particularly useful. The first is where you want to give some of your assets to the next generation but your wife or husband will carry on needing the income from, or use of, those assets. One way around this is to leave the assets in trust, giving your spouse an interest in possession during his or her lifetime, with your children (or perhaps their children) holding the reversionary interest (see page 128). But note that, while this ensures that your assets are used largely as you would wish, it does not have any IHT advantage. This is because, under IHT, a person with an interest in possession is deemed to own the underlying trust assets and to give them away when the interest ends. So there could be a large IHT bill at the time of the second death. You could avoid this problem by using a discretionary trust instead, with both your spouse and your children named as beneficiaries. This would be tax-efficient provided the transfer of assets into the trust was covered by your tax-free slice or one of the other exemptions.

However, an interest-in-possession trust can be useful for IHT planning if assets are being passed to subsequent generations. This is because a reversionary interest does not count as part of a person's estate and so there is no IHT liability if it is transferred to someone else. If your children held the reversionary interest in a trust, they could easily transfer this interest to their own children if they wished to do so, without incurring any IHT liability.

The second important planning use of will trusts is where you are passing on your business. Rather than pass total control to, for example, a relatively inexperienced son or daughter, or to a spouse who is not involved in the business, it may make sense to put the land or property used by the business into trust. Provided the owner qualifies for business property relief or agricultural property relief, the trust will also qualify (see page 110). This is a complex area and you should seek the advice of your accountant and/or solicitor.

Note that a trust set up under your will is deemed to start on the date of death, so do not fall into the trap of setting up several trusts including one or more discretionary trusts under your will. A way round this would be to set up the discretionary trust(s) before death, putting in just a token amount to get them started and then adding more in your will.

Making loans

One way to 'freeze' the value of part of your estate is to make an interest-free loan to someone and leave him or her to keep the proceeds from investing the loan. A condition of the loan would normally be that it is repayable on demand. From your point of view, this is more secure than making an outright gift and can be a useful arrangement if you are unsure whether or not you will need the money back at some time in the future.

Of course, there is little point demanding repayment of a loan if the borrower simply does not have the money available to repay you. An even more secure route would be to make the loan to a discretionary trust and to name the intended recipient as a potential beneficiary under the trust.

'Associated operations'

Beware! Different transactions (gifts, loans, leases, and so on) that affect the same assets can be deemed to be linked together – in which case, they are called 'associated operations'. This could result in a complicated 'gift' being disallowed for tax purposes if the Inland Revenue decides that a series of transactions are designed mainly as a way of evading a tax bill. The legislation lists the following examples where transactions will not be treated as linked:

- if you arrange a lease, for example, giving you the right to live in a house, and you pay the full market rate for that lease, this will not be linked with any other transaction that takes place more than three years after the lease was made
- no transaction made on or after 27 March 1974 can be linked to a transaction made before that date.

You should also be aware that where a gift is made as a result of a series of associated operations over a period of time, for IHT purposes, the transfer will be considered to have taken place on the date of the last of the linked transactions – you will get relief against any tax paid at the earlier stages. This is an important point in relation to the size of your running total of gifts.

Using life insurance

There are three main ways in which life insurance can be a useful inheritance planning tool:

- covering the potential tax bill on a PET
- making a gift which builds up outside your estate
- covering an expected tax bill on your estate.

These are discussed in turn below. All rely on making use of two factors:

- *Tax-free gifts* Taking out insurance for the benefit of someone else means that the premiums count as gifts. You can ensure that there is no possibility of IHT on these premiums if you make sure they count as tax-free gifts. The most commonly used exemptions are to make the premiums out of your normal income or to ensure that they fall within your yearly tax-free exemption of £3,000.
- *Trust status* If the proceeds of an insurance policy are payable to you, the payout will be added to your estate when you die, which will increase the size of your estate and will cause delay before your beneficiaries have access to the payout. Therefore, it is important that the policy proceeds are paid direct to the intended beneficiary. You make sure this happens by 'writing' the insurance

policy 'in trust', which means that the policy is held in trust for the benefit of whomever you name and the proceeds are the property of that person rather than of you or your estate. Insurance companies will generally write a policy in trust for you at no extra charge (since they are able, in most cases, to use standard documents).

The cost of insurance increases with the likelihood of the insurance company having to pay out. So if you are in poor health, or very old, buying life insurance may be very expensive.

PETs and insurance

If you make a gift which counts as a PET, you may want to be absolutely sure that any IHT bill which subsequently arises could be paid. (Similarly, you might want to ensure that any extra tax on a chargeable gift arising on death could be paid.) One way of ensuring this would be to take out a 'term insurance' policy. Term insurance

---

EXAMPLE 14.3

In 1999–2000 Jeremy gives his niece, Penny, a gift of £10,000. It counts as a PET and so there is no tax to pay at the time of the gift. However, Jeremy's running total exceeds £231,000, and if he were to die within seven years of making the gift, Penny would face a demand for tax on the gift. The potential tax liability would be as follows:

Years between gift and death	% Rate of tax on the gift (at 1999–2000 tax rates)	Potential tax bill (£s)
Up to 3	40	4,000
More than 3 and up to 4	32	3,200
More than 4 and up to 5	24	2,400
More than 5 and up to 6	16	1,600
More than 6 up to 7	8	800
More than 7	no tax	0

Jeremy takes out a seven-year term insurance which would pay Penny £4,000 if he died within the first three years and a reducing sum thereafter to cover the tax bill which would arise.

---

pays out if you die within a specified time – in this case, seven years; should you survive the specified period, it pays out nothing. Since the liability for IHT on a PET decreases as the years go by, the cover you need can also reduce – in other words, you want 'decreasing term insurance'. See Example 14.3 on page 197.

Reducing the size of your estate

You could use life insurance to build up a gift which does not count as part of your estate. For example, you might use the full £3,000 yearly tax-free exemption to pay the premiums on a policy that will pay out to the recipient either after some specified period (in which case, you need an 'endowment policy' – see Glossary) or when you die (in which case, you need a 'whole life policy' – see Glossary).

In choosing this strategy, you will need to weigh it against alternative strategies: for example, setting up a trust which could invest in a wide range of assets. The 'up-front' costs of setting up your own trust will be higher, but the ongoing costs could work out to be less than for a life insurance policy. If you have relatively small sums to give, the insurance route would be more appropriate.

Paying IHT when you die

You could take out a whole life policy (which pays out *whenever* you die) to provide a lump sum to meet an expected IHT bill on your estate. In essence, this is no different from using insurance as a way of making a gift on death as already discussed, but the factors to consider are slightly different: you could save in your own investment fund (either within your estate or within a trust) to meet a potential IHT bill, but it would take time to build up the full amount needed. If you died in the meantime, your investment would be insufficient to cover the IHT. Taking out a whole life insurance policy removes that risk because (provided you have bought the appropriate level of cover) it would pay out the full amount needed whether you die sooner or later.

Using long-term care insurance

The longer you live, the greater the chance that you may suffer some infirmity in your old age. If you then need a carer to help you with day-to-day living or require continuous nursing care, this will inevitably be expensive. If your capital comes to less than £16,000 and your income is low, the state will currently pay some or all of the costs for you. If your capital is greater than this, you will have to pay out of your own pocket until the stage at which your capital has been run down to less than £16,000. If you had to move into a residential or nursing home and your husband or wife or a dependant would be left at home, the value of your house should not be included in the assessment of how much capital you own. But, if you had been living alone, your home would normally count as part of your capital and might have to be sold to cover the care fees.

You could consider long-term care insurance as a way of protecting your capital and, thus, the inheritance you want to pass on to your heirs. In brief, long-term care insurance pays out a regular sum towards the cost of care either in your own home or in a residential or nursing home if you can no longer carry out a given number of specified 'activities of daily living' (ADLs) for yourself. This saves you dipping into your capital or having to rely on means-tested state help. (For more on long-term care insurance and insurance in general, see *The Which? Guide to Insurance*.)

Gifts from the deathbed

If, say, you are seriously ill and do not expect to live for long, you might make a gift in contemplation of your death – known as a *donatio mortis causa*. Such a gift does not take effect until your death and it lapses completely if you do not die after all (or if the recipient dies before you).

In a situation as described above, should your intention be to make an outright gift to someone that is not conditional on your dying, it would be wise to set down your intention in writing – in, say, a signed letter to the recipient – to safeguard against the gift being mistakenly treated as a *donatio mortis causa* (and thus being treated as part of your estate if you survive).

A further point to watch out for, in a deathbed situation, is that a gift which is made by cheque is not made until the cheque has been *cleared* against the giver's account. If death takes place before then, the gift would become invalid.

Altering a will after death

Oddly enough, your will is not the final word in regard to your estate. Following death, there is a two-year period during which the will can be varied – in effect, rewritten – and your gifts reallocated. The allocation of the estate can also be varied where a person dies intestate (see Chapter 12).

The variation must be agreed by all the beneficiaries named under the will and is made by one or more of them who must complete a written deed. No beneficiary may receive any payment either in cash or kind in return for benefits given up due to the variation.

A variation can affect part, or the whole, of an estate, except that the amount an infant child would receive cannot be reduced without the consent of the court and the way in which assets put into trust are left may not be varied.

Where – as is usual – the redistribution affects the potential IHT due on the estate, an election must be made within six months of the deed of variation to the Inland Revenue for tax to be reassessed. In addition, if the variation would alter the CGT liability, an election can also be made to the Inland Revenue to reassess this. (Although there is no CGT on death, the personal representatives might have to sell assets after death, which could give rise to a CGT bill. And, if assets originally left to one beneficiary are to be passed instead to another, there could, in the absence of an election, be a CGT bill.)

There are, in fact, two ways in which the passing on of an estate can be varied: by deed of variation or by 'disclaimer'. The main difference between the two methods is that, under a deed of variation, who is to receive various assets can be changed from one person to another. Under a disclaimer, the named beneficiary in the will merely says he or she does not want the gift, in which case the assets are reallocated according to the terms of the will (for example, they might simply be added to the residue) or to the rules of intestacy. It follows from this that a disclaimer can only increase the share of the estate going to some or all of the other beneficiaries. By contrast, a deed of variation can be used to make gifts to people who did not originally stand to benefit from the will or intestacy.

Note that a disclaimer cannot be made if the original beneficiary has already received some benefit from the inherited assets that he or she intends to disclaim.

In considering whether or not to vary the way an estate is left, and the form that any variation should take, all the normal planning considerations come into play: for example, making sure the tax-free slice is used, choosing whether gifts should be free of tax or bear their own tax, creating or renouncing life interests and so on. See Example 14.4.

In the 1989 Budget, the government of the day announced its intention to restrict severely the possibilities for using deeds of variation (but not disclaimers). In the event, the proposal was dropped from the subsequent Finance Bill after concerns that, without the ability to vary wills, unwelcome pressure would tend to be brought to bear on people, when they were already under stress due to illness or old age, to sort out their affairs efficiently. Nevertheless, the then Conservative government said it would keep the matter under review and the current Labour government is more, rather than less, likely to tighten up the IHT regime, so there may be further attempts to reduce the use of deeds of variation. The message is clear: plan ahead so that variation is unnecessary.

EXAMPLE 14.4

When Fred died, his will revealed that he had left £500,000 to his wife, Betty, and the residue of his estate to his daughter, Linda. His daughter's share was £50,000 on which no tax was due, because Fred's taxable estate plus a couple of PETs made in the last seven years came to a running total of only £60,000.

Betty intends, when she dies, to leave everything to Linda, but this will mean a large IHT bill on an estate made up of Betty's own £20,000 or so and the £500,000 left to her by Fred. Assuming she had made no chargeable gifts in the seven years before death, tax of [£520,000 − £231,000 = £289,000] x 0.4 = £115,600 would be payable (based on 1999–2000 rates). But this bill could be reduced if some changes are made to Fred's will.

Betty does not need the whole £500,000, so she and Linda make a deed of variation directing that Fred's estate of £550,000 be split as follows: £221,000 to Linda – which, with the earlier PETs, uses up the whole of Fred's tax-free slice – and the residue of £329,000 to his wife. There is still no IHT to pay on Fred's estate, and the potential bill when Betty dies is reduced to [£329,000 + £20,000 − £231,000 = £118,000] x 0.4 = £47,200. This is a saving of £68,400.

Part 4

Your home

Chapter 15
Your home as a gift

A ROOF OVER YOUR HEAD

'If we gave the house to you now, Becky, it would mean a lot less tax to pay at the end of the day,' explained Joan. 'But where would you and Dad live? You surely wouldn't want to stay here with all our children around you?' quizzed Becky, trying hard to take in the whole idea. 'Good grief, no!' laughed Joan. 'That might not achieve the tax savings we had in mind anyway. No, Dad and I were planning on moving to the cottage. After all, we don't need to be in town these days. Well, what do you think?'

In essence, your home is no different from any other asset which you own. It can form part of your estate and can be the subject of a gift in much the same way as any other possession you own. As such, the bulk of this book applies to your home as much as to any other asset. However, because your home is likely to be your most valuable possession, it is worth drawing together here some of the points which should be borne in mind if you are contemplating making a gift of your home either as a lifetime gift or at the time of death.

Who owns what?

If you own your home jointly with someone else, it is important to think about how you own it. As discussed in Chapter 9, there are two forms of joint ownership (in England and Wales): joint tenancy and tenants in common.

If you own your own home as a joint tenant with someone else, you each have equal shares in the home and have identical rights to enjoy the whole home. On death, the share of the owner who dies passes automatically to the remaining co-owner(s). This is very simple and convenient and can be the best arrangement for married couples and other partners in stable relationships, especially if the value of their estates taken together is no more than the tax-free slice for inheritance tax (i.e. £231,000 in 1999–2000).

However, owning the home as tenants in common gives you greater flexibility and better scope for tax planning. Tenants in common still have the right to enjoy the whole home, but you each have distinct shares in the home which need not be equal and do not pass automatically to the other owners on death. Instead, the share of the home is passed on in accordance with your will or, if you hadn't made a will, the rules of intestacy.

We have already seen in Example 14.1 how failing to use the tax-free slice when the first partner of a married couple dies can result in an unnecessarily large tax bill when the second spouse dies. With ownership of the home arranged as tenants in common, it becomes possible for each spouse to arrange to use their tax-free slice by, for example, passing their share of the home on to their children, say, instead of to their wife or husband. This can save IHT overall, but is worth doing only if you can be sure that the surviving spouse will continue to have a secure home – for example, by giving him or her the protection of a formal tenancy agreement.

The importance of a will

Chapter 12 described the problems which can arise if you die intestate – i.e. without having made a will. These can be especially acute if your home is the main asset in your estate.

If you die without a will and you are survived by children or other relatives your husband or wife inherits outright only a certain part of your estate. He or she does have the right to opt to take his or her share of your estate in the form of the home rather than other assets. But what if that share of your estate is worth less than the home? The husband or wife may well find that part of the home has to be put into trust for the benefit of the children, say, or that more distant relatives insist on the sale of the home in order to release their own inheritance as cash.

The position of an unmarried partner is even worse. He or she may have no automatic right to share in your estate. If he or she has been your partner throughout the two years up to death or has been financially dependent on you, he or she can apply to the courts under the Inheritance (Provision for Family and Dependants) Act 1975. But the court can only make awards of income (which can be rolled up as a lump sum); it cannot direct that capital assets are distributed in one way or another.

Therefore, if the home is jointly held as tenants in common, it is essential that you make a will specifying how your share of the home is to be passed on.

Your home as a lifetime gift

If you expect your estate at death to exceed the tax-free slice, it would be very convenient if you could give away your home now in your lifetime. Making a gift of your home to your children, say, would count as a potentially exempt transfer (PET). There would be no IHT to pay at the time you made the gift and, provided you survived seven years, no IHT at all. There is, however, a small snag: if you give away your home, where do you intend to live? If you mean to stay in the home, the gift will not work for IHT purposes, because it will count as a gift with reservation (see page 108).

There are a couple of ways around this problem, though neither is very satisfactory. First, you could share the home with the people to whom you give it. Provided you all live together and share the running costs of the home, the gift should not count as one with reservation. But, if the recipients subsequently move out, the gift will become a gift with reservation – so make sure you don't fall out!

The second solution relies on the caveat that a gift is not a gift with reservation if you give full consideration in money or money's worth for the use you continue to make of the gift. For example, you could give away your house but buy a lease at the full market rate which lets you live in it for some specified period – for example, long enough to cover your expected remaining years, plus a few extra years to be on the safe side. Alternatively, you might offer your services as, for example, a housekeeper or gardener, provided the value of your work was equivalent to the market rent for the property you continue to occupy.

Change of plan

The only satisfactory way of giving your home as a lifetime gift is if you genuinely do have somewhere else to live – for example, a retirement cottage or moving in with friends or relatives. But suppose your circumstances change and you move back into the home you had previously given away? This could trigger the gift with reservation rules. However, if you become unable to maintain yourself because of old age, infirmity or some other reason and your moving back into your old home is a reasonable way for the recipient of the gift – who would have to be your relation or spouse – to provide care for you, the gift with reservation rule will not apply.

Watch out for CGT

Giving away your home does not normally trigger a CGT bill, because any gain on your only or main home is generally exempt. In some situations, however, there will be a CGT bill. These arise where:

- you have lived away from home for a time
- you have let out all or part of the home
- part of the home has been used exclusively for your work
- the garden was greater than the normal size for a home of that type (usually taken to be greater than half a hectare).

Keep your options open

Do not be in too much of a hurry to give away your home. People are tending to live longer but increasingly need some degree of professional care in their later years. This is very expensive and many people are surprised to find that the state foots the bill only if their income and assets are very low – see page 199. Taking out long-term care insurance, as described on pages 198–9, might be a solution. If not, the home which you had expected to pass on to your children might in the end be needed to fund nursing home or residential home fees. Your home can also be a valuable source of additional income if your resources become tight in later old age. Taking out a home income plan (usually a mortgage linked to an annuity) enables you to convert the capital in your home into a lifetime income.

Glossary

A word or phrase shown in *italics* has a separate entry in the Glossary.

accumulation-and-maintenance trust   A type of *discretionary trust* which enjoys special tax treatment: gifts to the trust count as *potentially exempt transfers*; there is no *inheritance tax* on the property within the trust nor when property is paid out to *beneficiaries*. The special treatment is only granted provided certain rules are kept: for example, at least one beneficiary must become entitled to part or all of the trust property by the age of 25. These trusts are especially useful as a way of giving to one or more young children, for example, grandchildren.

administrator   The *personal representative* who settles the affairs of someone who has died without leaving a will. He or she is appointed by the court and will often be the husband or wife of the deceased person.

affinity card   another name for *donation card*

allowable business expense   Spending you make in the course of running your business that can be set against the income of the business when working out the profits for income tax purposes. Generally, to count as allowable, the spending must have been made 'wholly and exclusively' for the purpose of the business.

Alternative Investment Market (AIM)   A stockmarket for fledgling companies which want to raise money by issuing shares to the public but at lower cost and with fewer restrictions than a listing on the main stockmarket would involve. Opened in 1995, it replaces the Unlisted Securities Market (USM) which is now closed to new entrants.

asset   Anything which you own: for example, your home, car, personal possessions, money, investments, and so on.

bare trust　Arrangement whereby someone holds property as nominee for someone else. For tax purposes, the ultimate beneficiary is treated as owning the property outright.

beneficiary　A person who may receive property from a trust, or who has been left something in a will.

bequest　A gift to someone in a will. Also called a *legacy*.

British Government stocks　A type of investment issued by the government which generally pays a regular income and a capital sum after a specified period of time. (Some stocks do not offer the capital sum, only income.) When you buy a British Government stock, you are, in effect, making a loan to the government. These are considered to be very secure investments because of the very low risk that the government would be unable to repay you. Also known as *gilts*.

CAF　Abbreviation for the *Charities Aid Foundation*.

capital gains tax (CGT)　Tax on gains that you make from selling an *asset* for more than it was worth when you first started to own it. If you give the asset away, you are deemed to have made a gain if the asset has risen in value over the time you have owned it. In practice, there is often no tax to pay on a gain because you are allowed to make various deductions in calculating the gain for tax purposes. The most important deductions are *indexation allowance,* CGT *taper relief* and the 'tax-free slice'. The tax-free slice enables you to make a given amount of otherwise taxable gains free of CGT. The rates at which tax is levied on taxable gains are 20 per cent and 40 per cent in 1999–2000.

CGT　Abbreviation for *capital gains tax.*

CGT taper relief　Reduction in the value of capital gains on which tax is charged. The reduction is given according to the number of complete tax years since 5 April 1998 you have held the asset on which the gain is realised.

chargeable transfer　A gift that is not a *potentially exempt transfer* and that is not tax-free for another reason (for example, if it were a gift between husband and wife), and on which there may be an *inheritance tax* bill.

charitable trust　A type of *trust* whose aims and purposes meet the requirements for charitable status. This means that there is no *income tax, capital gains tax* or *inheritance tax* on the trust property or payments from it provided they are used for charitable ends. (From 1999, however, charitable trusts will be unable to claim tax deducted from dividends on shares.) In addition, income tax relief is given on gifts to the trust provided they are made through one of the special schemes available – such as through a *covenant* or *Gift Aid*.

Charities Aid Foundation (CAF)   A charity whose aim is to promote and assist other charities. It is a rich source of information about charities and operates a Charity Account which provides individuals (and companies) with a tax-efficient and flexible method of giving to charity.

Charity Commission   The government department responsible for registering charities, investigating abuse of charitable status and helping charities to run efficiently and within the charity laws.

chattels   A tax term for those of your possessions which are physical and portable things: for example, jewellery, furniture, cars. Technically they are referred to as 'tangible movable property'.

children   This may be defined in various ways for the purpose of specific pieces of legislation. For example, under the *intestacy* rules, 'children' means children of your current marriage, children of any former marriage(s), illegitimate children and adopted children, but it does not include stepchildren. Under the *income tax* rules, 'children' is more widely defined and does include stepchildren.

codicil   An amendment to a *will* to be considered in conjunction with the will. If the amendments are many or complicated, it will usually be better to rewrite the will rather than use a codicil.

covenant   A legally binding agreement to make regular payments of income to a person or organisation. Before 15 March 1988, gifts to people and charities under a covenant could attract relief from *income tax*, but, from that date onwards, tax relief is restricted to covenanted gifts to charities. The precise wording of the covenant is important otherwise the covenant could fail to qualify for the tax relief.

deed of variation   See *variation*.

demonstrative legacy   A gift of money or things made under a *will* and to be provided out of a specified part of the deceased person's *estate*.

deposited deed   Another name for a *loan covenant*.

deposited covenant   Another name for a *loan covenant*.

disabled trust   A type of *discretionary trust*, qualifying for special tax treatment, for the maintenance or other benefit of a mentally disabled person (as defined under the Mental Health Act 1983). Gifts to the trust by the disabled person are free of *inheritance tax* and gifts by other people to the trust count as *potentially exempt transfers (PETs)*; property held within the trust is free of *inheritance tax*, as are payments to the disabled person; the disabled person is treated as owning the trust property and thus if he or she gives it away the gift counts as a PET.

disclaimer   The voluntary giving up of a gift made to you under a *will* following the death of the giver. The gift is then distributed according to the other terms of the will (for example, it might increase the value of the *residue*).

discretionary trust   A *trust* in which none of the beneficiaries has an *interest in possession* and the distribution of trust property or income from it is at the discretion of the *trustees*. The tax treatment of this type of trust is not as favourable as the regime for other trusts: gifts to a discretionary trust count as *chargeable transfers*; the trust fund is subject to *income tax*, *capital gains tax* and *inheritance tax (IHT)* with IHT being levied every ten years according to a complex formula; there is also IHT to pay on payments from the trust to the beneficiaries.

domicile   The country or state which is considered to be your permanent home in the sense that it is the place where you would expect to end your days. It is not necessarily the place where you live at present. The term is imprecise and not defined in any Act of Parliament.

donation card   A credit card which, when used, generates donations to charity. The card-issuing company usually agrees to make a donation when you first take out a card and then further donations each time you use it. In other respects, the card is like a normal credit card.

endowment policy   A type of life insurance policy which builds up an investment value over a specified term (the 'endowment' period). At the end of the term, the policy matures and the investment can be cashed in. Earlier encashment is possible, but returns may be low.

Enterprise Investment Scheme (EIS)   A tax-efficient scheme for investing in the shares of new unquoted companies (including *Alternative Investment Market* companies). Various reliefs from income tax and capital gains tax are given, provided certain conditions are met.

estate   All a person's possessions – home, car, money, investments, and so on – less their debts.

excluded property   Possessions and assets which are outside the scope of *inheritance tax*, for example, a *reversionary interest* in trust property (in most cases), certain government stocks if you are *domiciled* and *resident* outside the UK.

executor   The *personal representative* who sorts out the affairs of someone who has died in accordance with their *will* (and any subsequent *variation* to it). The executor will normally be a person (or company) appointed by the deceased person in his/her will.

family provision claim   A claim by someone who, in the first instance, does not benefit from your *estate*, either under the terms of your *will* or under the *intestacy* rules, for financial support from the estate. The claimant will need to show that he or she was dependent on you during your lifetime or that he or she was an unmarried partner living with you as husband or wife throughout the two years prior to your death.

fixed-interest trust   Another name for an *interest-in-possession trust*.

friendly society plans   A type of investment, basically the same as some investment-type *life insurance* but which qualifies for special tax treatment. You pay premiums to the society that are invested for a given time, after which you receive a pay out. There is no *income tax* or *capital gains tax* on the investment fund and there is no tax on the pay-out. The sum you can invest in these plans is restricted to a relatively low amount.

gift with reservation   This occurs when you give away something but retain the right to use or enjoy the thing: for example, you might give away your home but continue to live there, or give away a piece of furniture but continue to keep it in your home. For *inheritance tax* purposes, a gift with reservation does not count as a gift at the time it is made but continues to be part of your estate. Tax becomes due (if payable) at the time the reservation stops: for example, on death. It is possible to make an outright gift and for the reservation to arise some time after the gift is made (for example, if you move back into a home you gave away).

Gift Aid   A special scheme for use in making lump sum gifts to charity of £250 or more. The gift qualifies for tax relief at your top rate of *income tax*. See also *Millennium Gift Aid*.

'gilts'   Another name for *British Government stocks*.

gross   Used in the context of tax computations to mean 'before tax'.

gross covenant   A legally binding agreement to make annual payments to a person or body – e.g. a charity. Under the agreement, the person or body receives a fixed sum – i.e. if the payments are to a charity and so qualify for tax relief, the sum you pay will vary if the tax rate varies.

'grossing-up'   The process of finding out the before-tax amount of a payment from the *net* amount. The 'grossed-up' value is the sum of the net value plus the amount of tax which has been paid (or deemed to have been paid). Grossing-up is carried out by dividing the net sum by $[1 - (tax\ rate \div 100)]$. For example, take net income of £77 which has been taxed at the basic rate of *income tax* of 23 per cent. The grossed-up value is: £77 $\div [1 - (23 \div 100)] = £77 \div [1 - 0.23] = £77 \div 0.77 = £100$. In other words, tax of £23 has been paid and the grossed-up value is the sum of £77 + £23.

hold-over relief   The process of deferring a *capital gains tax* bill due at the time a gift is made by passing the liability to the recipient of the gift. This is done by deducting from the recipient's *initial value* of the gift the amount of tax otherwise payable.

IHT   Abbreviation for *inheritance tax*.

income tax   Tax payable on most types of income: for example, earnings from a job, interest on investments, and so on. Everyone has a personal allowance (£4,335 in the 1999–2000 tax year), which means that income of up to that amount is tax-free. Other allowances and deductions may also apply. Tax is charged at a lower rate of 10 per cent, a basic rate of 23 per cent and a higher rate of 40 per cent in the 1999–2000 tax year. A special savings rate of 20 per cent applies to interest and similar income from many types of savings and investments.

independent taxation   System of taxing married couples introduced from 6 April 1990 under which husband and wife are treated as separate units for *income tax* and *capital gains tax* purposes. This means, for example, that they each have their own personal allowance and basic-rate tax band. (Under the earlier system, income and gains of the wife were generally treated for tax as being those of the husband.)

indexation allowance   That part of a capital gain on an *asset* that is judged to be due to the asset's value keeping pace with inflation (either since you first owned it or since March 1982, whichever date is later). This part of the gain is not liable for *capital gains tax (CGT)* and is deducted from the capital gain in calculating any CGT liability. Indexation allowance is available only for periods up to April 1998. After that time, it is replaced by *CGT taper relief*.

Individual Savings Account (ISA)   Tax-efficient savings scheme introduced from 6 April 1999 through which you can invest in, for example, bank and building society accounts, shares, unit trusts and life insurance products.

inheritance tax (IHT)   Tax due on a *chargeable transfer* either in your lifetime or when your *estate* is passed on at the time of death. Tax is worked out by looking at the running total of all such transfers over the last seven years. If this total comes to more than the tax-free slice (of £231,000 in the 1999–2000 tax year), tax will be payable. IHT is charged at a rate of 20 per cent on chargeable transfers made during your life (though extra tax may be due if you die within seven years) and at a rate of 40 per cent on transfers at the time of death.

interest in possession   The right to receive income from trust property. You may also have the right to receive the capital at some specified time or this may pass then to someone else.

interest-in-possession trust   A type of *trust* where one or more *beneficiaries* have the right to receive the income from the trust property at the time the income arises (called an *interest in possession*). The same person or someone else may have the right to the trust property when the trust comes to an end (called the *reversionary interest*). The tax treatment of this type of trust is fairly favourable: gifts paid into the trust count as *potentially exempt transfers (PETs)*; there is no *inheritance tax* on the trust property or on the income payments from it; the person holding the interest in possession is treated as owning the trust property, so when the trust comes to an end, that person is deemed to make a PET.

intestacy   Dying without having made a *will*. Your *estate* is distributed according to the rules of intestacy. These rules aim to protect your husband or wife up to a certain degree and your children. But the application of the rules can cause problems with, for example, part of your estate going to relatives outside the immediate family, or an unmarried partner being left nothing (though he or she would be eligible to make a *family provision claim*).

investment trust   A type of investment where you buy shares in a company whose business is investing in other companies and/or other assets.

ISA   Abbreviation for *Individual Savings Account*.

joint tenancy   A way of sharing the ownership of an *asset*. You and the other joint tenant(s) have equal shares in the property and the same rights to enjoy the use of the whole asset. You cannot sell or give away your share of the asset independently of the other joint tenant(s) and on death your share automatically passes to them.

life interest   The right to receive the income from an *asset* for as long as you live but not the asset itself. On your death, the asset passes to whoever has the *reversionary interest*.

loan covenant   A combination of a *covenant* and a loan that enables a gift to charity to benefit from the tax advantages of a covenant, but you give a single lump sum rather than committing yourself to regular payments over a number of years.

long-term care insurance   Insurance which pays out if you are unable to care for yourself. It helps you meet the cost of outside care either in your own home or in a residential or nursing home and is useful as a way of protecting capital which you hope to pass on as an inheritance.

Millennium Gift Aid   Temporary scheme to encourage giving to charities which support education and poverty-aid programmes in the world's poorest countries. From 31 July 1998 to 31 December 2000, tax relief at your top rate is available on such gifts of £100 or more (or a series of gifts together totalling £100 or more).

National Savings investments   A group of 'deposit-type' investments that are issued by the government. You invest and either receive a tax-free return or receive an income paid before the deduction of income tax. They include: National Savings Investment Accounts, National Savings Certificates, the Children's Bonus Bonds and National Savings Income Bonds.

net   Used in the context of tax computations to mean 'after tax has been deducted'.

net assets   Your *assets* less your debts and outstanding expenses.

net covenant   A legally binding agreement to make annual payments to a person or body – e.g. a charity. Under the agreement, you agree to pay a fixed sum – i.e. if the payments are to a charity and so qualify for tax relief, the overall sum the charity receives will vary if the tax rate varies.

Payroll Deduction   Another name for *Payroll Giving*.

Payroll Giving   A special scheme for making gifts to charity directly out of your earnings from a job. The gifts qualify for relief from *income tax* at your top rate.

pecuniary legacy   A gift in a *will* of a specified sum of money.

PEP   Abbreviation for *Personal Equity Plan*.

Personal Equity Plan (PEP)   An investment in shares, unit trusts, investment trusts and/or some types of bonds where the income and gains are free of *income tax* and *capital gains tax*, respectively, as long as the investments remain in the PEP. No new PEPs can be taken out after 5 April 1999.

personal representative   The person (or company) who sorts out the *estate* of someone who has died. There are two types of representative: the *administrator* who acts when there is no *will* and the *executor* who acts when there is a will.

PET   Abbreviation for *potentially exempt transfer*.

potentially exempt transfer (PET)   A gift between individuals or a gift between an individual and a *trust*, other than a *discretionary trust*, made during the lifetime of the giver. There is no *inheritance tax* charge on the gift provided the giver survives for seven years. If they do not, the PET is reassessed as a *chargeable transfer* and tax may then be due after all.

purchased life annuity   An investment whereby you hand over a lump sum to an insurer, which then pays you an income for life. You cannot get back your investment in the form of a lump sum, but part of each regular payment to you is deemed to be return of your capital – the rest is deemed to be income. The capital element of each payment does not count as income for tax purposes, so there is no *income tax* on that part and it cannot be used to make 'regular payments out of income' under the inheritance tax rules.

registered charity   A charity listed on the Register of Charities kept by the *Charity Commission*. Registration tells you that the charity met the criteria for charitable status at the time it applied for registration, but should not be regarded as a 'seal of approval'.

residence   The country or state which you currently make your home. 'Ordinarily resident' means that you make your home there year after year. 'Resident' may refer to a shorter-term home, e.g. while you are posted abroad. The terms are imprecise and are not defined in any Act of Parliament.

residuary gift   The gift under your *will* of whatever is left after all the *specific gifts* have been made, and debts and expenses (including tax) paid.

residue   Whatever is left after all the *specific gifts* have been made, and debts and expenses (including tax) paid.

Retail Prices Index   The government index which tracks the general cost of living. Changes in the index give a widely used measure of inflation.

reversionary interest   The right to the property in a *trust* at some specified time or on a specified occurrence, but not the right to income from or use of, the property before that time.

settlor   The person who sets up a *trust* and puts money or *assets* into it.

single-premium life insurance bond   A type of investment whereby you use a lump sum to buy an insurance policy. The life-cover element is low and the main aim of the policy is to provide investment growth. Special tax rules enable you to withdraw money periodically from the bond but to defer any liability for *income tax* on the withdrawals until later. These withdrawals do not count as income for the purpose of the 'regular payments out of income' exemption from *inheritance tax* on gifts.

specific gift   Gifts of money or things under a *will*. The gifts can be of various types: for example, a named item, a type of *asset*, a *pecuniary legacy* or a *demonstrative legacy*.

survivorship destination   An arrangement under Scottish law which ensures that, on the death of a joint owner of property, his or her share of the property passes automatically to the surviving co-owner(s), even if the deceased person's *will* specifies otherwise.

taper relief   Tax relief which reduces the amount of *inheritance tax* due on a *potentially exempt transfer (PET)* or *chargeable transfer* which is reassessed following the death of the giver within seven years of making the gift. The size of the relief increases with the elapse of time from making of the gift. Taper relief *does not* reduce extra tax due on an *estate* as a result of PETs being reassessed. (Do not confuse this form of taper relief with the new *CGT taper relief*.)

tenancy in common   A method of jointly owning an *asset*, where you and the other owners have specified shares of the asset which you can sell or give away without the agreement of the other owners. On death, your share is given away in accordance with your *will* or the rules of *intestacy*.

testator   The person (strictly, a man) who makes a *will*.

testatrix   A woman who makes a *will*.

trust   A legal arrangement whereby property is held by *trustees* on behalf of one or more *beneficiaries* to be used in accordance with the rules of the trust and trust law. Trusts can be very useful when making gifts as a way of giving *assets* but retaining some control over the way in which the assets are used; they are also useful if you wish to split the income and capital of assets and give each to a different person (or group of people).

trustee   A person who is responsible for investing and distributing *trust* property in accordance with the rules of the trust and trust law. The trustees of a trust are the owners of the trust property but they hold it for the benefit of the *beneficiaries* and not their own use.

variation   The process of changing the gifts made under a *will* after the *testator/testatrix* has died. This is achieved by a 'deed of variation' drawn up by one or more of the *beneficiaries*.

Venture Capital Trust (VCT)   A tax-efficient scheme for investing in a *trust* company whose purpose is to invest in the shares or securities of unquoted companies. Various reliefs from *income tax* and *capital gains tax* are given, provided certain conditions are met.

whole life policy   A type of life insurance policy designed to pay out on the death of the policyholder whenever that might occur. Policies can also cover more than one person with payment due on either the first or second death.

will   A legal document specifying how your *estate* is to be distributed and to whom at the time of death.

Addresses

Gifts to charities

The Central Register of Charities
Web site:
www.charity-commission.gov.uk

**The Charities Aid Foundation
(CAF)**
Kings Hill, West Malling,
Kent ME19 4TA
Tel: (01732) 520000
Fax: (01732) 520001
Web site: www.charitynet.org

**The Charity Commission for
England and Wales**
St Albans House,
57–60 Haymarket,
London SW1Y 4QX
Tel: 0171-210 4477
Fax: 0171-210 4545

**The Charity Commission for
England and Wales**
Second floor, 20 Kings Parade,
Queens Dock, Liverpool L3 4DQ
Tel: 0151-703 1500
Fax: 0151-703 1555

**The Charity Commission for
England and Wales**
Woodfield House, Tangier,
Taunton, Somerset SO14 2GD
Tel: 0870 333 0123
Fax: (01823) 345003

Inland Revenue
(for charities in England, Wales
and Northern Ireland)
Financial Intermediaries and
Claims Office (FICO) *and*
Charities Repayment Office,
St John's, Merton Road, Bootle,
Merseyside L69 9BB
Tel: 0151-472 6000
also:
FICO Nottingham, PO Box 46,
Nottingham NG2 1BD
Tel: 0115-974 0000
Helpline: 0115-974 2000
Fax: 0115-974 1863

Inland Revenue
(for charities in Scotland)
FICO Scotland, Trinity Park
House, South Trinity Road,
Edinburgh EH5 3SD
Tel: 0131-551 8127
Minicom: 0131-552 0622
Fax: 0131-551 8127

Inland Revenue
Web site: www.open.gov.uk/inrev

**National Council for Voluntary
Organisations (NCVO)**
(for England)
Regent's Wharf,
8 All Saints Street,
London N1 9RL
Tel: 0171-713 6161
Fax: 0171-713 6300
Email: ncvo@ncvo-vol.org.uk
Web site: www.ncvo-vol.org.uk

**Northern Ireland Council for
Voluntary Action (NICVA)**
127 Ormeau Road,
Belfast BT7 1SH
Tel: (01232) 321224
Fax: (01232) 438350
Email:
info.nicva.cinni@nics. gov.uk
Web site: www.nicva.org

**Scottish Council for Voluntary
Organisations (SCVO)**
18 Claremont Crescent,
Edinburgh EH7 4AN
Tel: 0131-556 3882
Fax: 0131-556 0279
Email: scvo.general@
gunna. almac.co.uk

**Wales Council for Voluntary
Action (WCVA)**
Llysifor, Crescent Road,
Caerphilly CF83 1XL
Tel: (01222) 855100
Email: wcva@mcr1.poptel.org.uk

Gifts to family and friends

**Capital Taxes Office (England
and Wales)**
Ferrers House, PO Box 38,
Castle Meadow Road,
Nottingham NG2 1BB
Tel: 0115-974 2400
Fax: 0115-974 2432

**Capital Taxes Office (Northern
Ireland)**
Dorchester House,
52–58 Great Victoria Street,
Belfast BT2 7QL
Tel: (01232) 505353
Fax: (01232) 505305

Capital Taxes Office (Scotland)
Mulberry House, 16 Picardy
Place, Edinburgh EH1 3NB
Tel: 0131-524 3000
Fax: 0131-556 9894

Capital Taxes Office
Web site: www.cto.eds.co.uk

Office for National Statistics
1 Drummond Gate,
London SW1V 2QQ
Public Enquiry Point:
0171-533 6262

Retail Prices Index and indexation factors

Local tax offices and Tax Enquiry Centres: refer to local telephone directories under 'Inland Revenue'.

To find an accountant

The following professional bodies can provide a list of members:

Association of Chartered Certified Accountants

29 Lincoln's Inn Fields,
London WC2A 3EE
Tel: 0171-396 5900
Fax: 0171-813 8054
Email: services.enquiries@acca.co.uk
Web site: www.acca.co.uk

Institute of Chartered Accountants in England and Wales

PO Box 433, Chartered Accountants' Hall, Moorgate Place, London EC2P 2BJ
Tel: 0171-920 8100
Fax: 0171-920 0547
Email: comms@icaew.co.uk
Web site: www.icaew.co.uk

Institute of Chartered Accountants in Ireland

Chartered Accountants' House,
87–89 Pembroke Road,
Ballsbridge, Dublin 4
Tel: (00 353) 1 668 0400
Fax: (00 353) 1 668 0842
Email: ca@icai.ie
Web site: www.icai.ie

Institute of Chartered Accountants of Scotland

27 Queen Street,
Edinburgh EH2 1LA
Tel: 0131-225 5673
Fax: 0131-225 3813
Web site: www.icas.org.uk

To find a solicitor

The following professional bodies can provide a list of members:

The Law Society

113 Chancery Lane,
London WC2A 1PL
Tel: 0171-242 1222
Web site: www.lawsociety.org.uk

The Law Society of Northern Ireland

Law Society House,
90 Victoria Street,
Belfast, BT1 3GN
Tel: (01232) 231614
Fax: (01232) 232606

The Law Society of Scotland

26 Drumsheugh Gardens,
Edinburgh EH3 7YR
Tel: 0131-226 7411
Fax: 0131-225 2934
Email: lawscot@lawscot.org.uk
Web site: www.lawscot.org.uk

The Office for the Supervision of Solicitors

Victoria Court,
8 Dormer Place,
Leamington Spa,
Warwickshire CV32 5AE
Tel: (01926) 820082
Fax: (01926) 431435

The Society of Trust and Estate Practitioners (STEP)
108 Jermyn Street,
London SW1Y 6EE
Tel: 0171-839 3886
Fax: 0171-839 3669

Ombudsman

Banking Ombudsman
70 Gray's Inn Road,
London WC1X 8NB
Tel: 0171-404 9944
Fax: 0171-405 5052
Email: banking.ombudsman@
obo.org.uk
Web site: www.obo.org.uk

Building Societies Ombudsman
Millbank Tower, Millbank,
London SW1P 4XS
Tel: 0171-931 0044
Fax: 0171-931 8485

Wills

Institute of Professional Willwriters
14 Foregate Street,
Worcester WR1 1DH
Tel: (01905) 611165
Fax: (01905) 726677

Society of Will Writers
91 Holme Drive, Sudbrooke,
Lincoln LN2 2SF
Tel: (01522) 595522
Freephone (helpline):
(0800) 838 270
Fax: (01522) 595110
Email: society.willwriters@
virgin.net
Web site: freespace.virgin.net/
society.willwriters

Willwriter's Association
Dolben Hall,
St Asaph, Denbighshire
LL17 0HN
Tel: (01745) 584414
Fax: (01745) 582006
Email: wills@lawyers-assoc.com
Web site: www.lawyers-assoc.com

Index

Page references in **bold type** indicate an entry in the Glossary

WHICH? BOOKS

The following titles were available as this book went to press.

General reference (legal, financial, practical, etc.)

Be Your Own Financial Adviser
401 Legal Problems Solved
150 Letters that Get Results
The Which? Guide to an Active Retirement
The Which? Guide to Changing Careers
The Which? Guide to Choosing a Career
The Which? Guide to Computers
The Which? Guide to Computers for Small Businesses
The Which? Guide to Divorce
The Which? Guide to Domestic Help
The Which? Guide to Employment
The Which? Guide to Gambling
The Which? Guide to Getting Married
The Which? Guide to Giving and Inheriting
The Which? Guide to Home Safety and Security
The Which? Guide to Insurance
The Which? Guide to the Internet
The Which? Guide to Money
The Which? Guide to Pensions
The Which? Guide to Renting and Letting
The Which? Guide to Shares
The Which? Guide to Starting Your Own Business
The Which? Guide to Working from Home
Which? Way to Beat the System
Which? Way to Clean It
Which? Way to Buy, Sell and Move House
Which? Way to Buy, Own and Sell a Flat
Which? Way to Save and Invest
Which? Way to Save Tax
What to Do When Someone Dies
Wills and Probate

Action Pack (A5 wallet with forms and 28-page book inside)

Make Your Own Will

Health

Understanding HRT and the Menopause
The Which? Guide to Complementary Medicine
The Which? Guide to Children's Health
The Which? Guide to Managing Asthma
The Which? Guide to Managing Back Trouble
The Which? Guide to Managing Stress
The Which? Guide to Men's Health
The Which? Guide to Women's Health
Which? Medicine

Gardening

The Gardening Which? Guide to Patio and Container
   Plants
The Gardening Which? Guide to Small Gardens
The Gardening Which? Guide to Successful Perennials
The Gardening Which? Guide to Successful Propagation
The Gardening Which? Guide to Successful Pruning
The Gardening Which? Guide to Successful Shrubs

Do-it-yourself

The Which? Book of Do-It-Yourself
The Which? Book of Home Improvements
The Which? Book of Plumbing and Central Heating
The Which? Book of Wiring and Lighting
The Which? Guide to Painting and Decorating
The Which? HomePlanner
Which? Way to Fix It

Travel/leisure

The Good Bed and Breakfast Guide
The Good Food Guide
The Good Skiing and Snowboarding Guide
The Which? Guide to Country Pubs
The Which? Guide to the Dordogne, the Lot and the Tarn
The Which? Guide to Weekend Breaks in Britain
The Which? Guide to Scotland
Which? Holiday Destination
The Which? Hotel Guide
The Which? Wine Guide

Ringbinder with looseleaf pages and plastic wallet

Great Days Out

Available from bookshops, and by post from
Which?, Dept TAZM, Castlemead,
Gascoyne Way, Hertford X, SG14 1LH

You can also order using your credit card
by phoning FREE on (0800) 252100
(quoting Dept TAZM)

Wills and Probate

If you die without making a will your wealth could go to the very person you least want to have it and your loved ones could lose out, perhaps to the Inland Revenue.

The practical, easy-to-follow advice contained in *Wills and Probate* has already helped thousands of people to make their wills. Whether you are single, married, divorced or co-habiting, it will show you how to write your will in such a way that your wishes can be carried out without any complications. The book not only provides sample text, but demonstrates how to change it at a later date.

The second part of the book covers probate: the administration of the estate of someone who has died. The book will enable you to decide whether you can execute the will confidently by yourself or whether you should call on professional help. A detailed case history runs through this section, including draft letters to exemplify the various points made.

Covering the law and procedure in England and Wales, and outlining the main differences which apply in Scotland and Northern Ireland, this revised edition highlights changes in government policy towards inheritance and describes what happens if there is no will.

Paperback   216 x 135mm   240 pages   £10.99

Available from bookshops, and by post from
Which?, Dept TAZM, Castlemead,
Gascoyne Way, Hertford X, SG14 1LH

You can also order using your credit card
by phoning FREE on (0800) 252100
(quoting Dept TAZM)

Make Your Own Will

If you die without leaving a will, your property may go to people you would prefer not to have it. And, just as galling, the Inland Revenue may end up taking a larger slice of your wealth than if you had taken control of your affairs.

This Pack takes you through the various stages in drawing up a will, explaining in plain English what to do and highlighting some of the pitfalls to avoid.

Inside the Pack you will find:

* step-by-step guidance on how to work out what you want in your will
* four different kinds of will form, with advice on choosing the one that is appropriate for your needs (or on whether you should get your will drawn up professionally)
* tips on choosing executors and on making proper plans to pay minimal inheritance tax
* advice on amending your will at a later date.

The pack is based on the law as it applies in England and Wales and is not suitable for people living in Scotland or Northern Ireland.

Paperback 234 x 155mm
28 pages plus forms & worksheets £10.99

Available from bookshops, and by post from
Which?, Dept TAZM, Castlemead,
Gascoyne Way, Hertford X, SG14 1LH

You can also order using your credit card
by phoning FREE on (0800) 252100
(quoting Dept TAZM)

Be Your Own Financial Adviser

Financial advice, like any other advice, can be good, bad or indifferent. But armed with the right facts, and some basic techniques, you can be your own financial adviser. This guide shows you how to clarify your financial needs and create a financial plan to meet them, just as a personal adviser would do for you.

Be Your Own Financial Adviser profiles the different products (investments, savings, insurance, loans) available, shows you how they can fit into your financial plan, how to choose the type best suited to you and where to get current information about them. It alerts you to any areas where you could be losing out, such as having savings in uncompetitive accounts, or where you are taking unnecessary risks with investments.

The book also lists the points to check out when you're talking to providers of financial products or financial advisers and how to interpret the information you're given. Simply written and full of useful tips and warnings, the book puts you in charge of your financial destiny.

Paperback   216 x 135mm   352 pages   £9.99

Available from bookshops, and by post from
Which?, Dept TAZM, Castlemead,
Gascoyne Way, Hertford X, SG14 1LH

You can also order using your credit card
by phoning FREE on (0800) 252100
(quoting Dept TAZM)

The Which? Guide to Shares

In Britain, nearly one adult in every three has become a share-owner, having responded to privatisation issues and, more recently, windfall shares from building society conversions. If you already have one or two shareholdings, or you are considering shares for the first time, this book will show you how these fascinating and versatile investments can help you achieve your financial ambitions.

It covers the role of shares in financial planning; how to buy and sell shares in the high street, through a traditional broker, or over the Internet; the range of shares available; risk – and how to turn it to your advantage; how shares are taxed, and how, legitimately, to avoid tax; portfolios for every pocket; the perks that accompany some shares; mastering rights issues, takeover bids, and so on; and how to play the stock market without even buying any shares.

The Which? Guide to Shares is a detailed introduction to the intriguing, fun and potentially rewarding world of share ownership, complete with extensive glossary and a useful address section.

Paperback   216 x 135mm   256 pages   £9.99

Available from bookshops, and by post from Which?, Dept TAZM, Castlemead, Gascoyne Way, Hertford X, SG14 1LH

You can also order using your credit card by phoning FREE on (0800) 252100 (quoting Dept TAZM)

The Which? Guide to Insurance

Insurance – the buying and selling of risk – is big business. Every year consumers spend billions of pounds on their policies. But how much of it do they really need and could they be paying less for any of it?

The Which? Guide to Insurance explains what to take into consideration before buying insurance so that you can avoid under- and over-insuring, and duplicating, and points out what to look for in the small print. It covers the range of policies from house contents and buildings to travel, health and car insurance. It also examines insurance, including life insurance, as an investment.

Using a no-nonsense, step-by-step approach, this guide shows you how to: work out how much insurance you need; buy the right insurance for your circumstances; cut the cost of your current insurance policies; make payments in the most cost-effective way; keep your insurance up to date; complain if your claim is unreasonably rejected.

Sound, money-saving tips on what to insure and how, plus tried and tested advice on how to take on an insurance company and win, with case histories to illustrate, make this book a great investment for anyone who needs insurance.

Paperback   216 x 135mm   320 pages   £10.99

Available from bookshops, and by post from
Which?, Dept TAZM, Castlemead,
Gascoyne Way, Hertford X, SG14 1LH

You can also order using your credit card
by phoning FREE on (0800) 252100
(quoting Dept TAZM)

Which? Way to Save and Invest

Whether you've got £50 or £5,000 to play with, it pays to pick the right investment. Many more people are shareholders as a result of privatisations and building society conversions. But deciding what to do with your spare cash can be a daunting task. You want to make sure that your dependants are protected and that you are prepared for the future, for retirement and for any emergency.

This book helps you to work out an overall investment strategy to suit your financial circumstances and ensure that you make the most of your savings. Written in straightforward language, it covers all the important areas of saving and investing from the traditional choices such as National Savings and banks, to unit trusts, investment trusts and commodities. Tax-efficient savings and investments are highlighted in a separate chapter.

Paperback   210 x 120mm   416 pages   £14.99

Available from bookshops, and by post from
Which?, Dept TAZM, Castlemead,
Gascoyne Way, Hertford X, SG14 1LH

You can also order using your credit card
by phoning FREE on (0800) 252100
(quoting Dept TAZM)

Which? Way to Save Tax

With self-assessment in place and a new tax regime in operation, the taxpayer now, more than ever, needs guiding through the complexities of the British tax system. *Which? Way to Save Tax*, fully updated each year to reflect Budget changes, helps you to ensure that you are paying the right amount of tax.

Written for the non-specialist, this book helps you to understand and make the most of the new tax rules. It guides investors through the overhaul of capital gains tax – essential reading for the millions of new shareholders created by the conversion of building societies to banks – and explains the biggest shake-up in tax-free investment for over a decade. It offers reliable and independent advice on tax as it affects employment, families, homes, investments, inheritance, pensions and the self-assessment regime.

Which? Way to Save Tax contains the answers to common tax questions, and should also help you work out whether some of the estimated billions of pounds of overpaid tax belong to you.

Paperback   210 x 120mm   352 pages   £14.99

Available from bookshops, and by post from
Which?, Dept TAZM, Castlemead,
Gascoyne Way, Hertford X, SG14 1LH

You can also order using your credit card
by phoning FREE on (0800) 252100
(quoting Dept TAZM)